C000264324

Acknowledgements
Information in this publication was researched and compiled by
John Wheeler who would like to thank the Bradbeer and
MacBeth families and those members of Calcot Park Golf Club
for their invaluable contributions, without which this book could
not have been printed.

Every effort has been made to ensure accuracy but the
publishers cannot accept any responsibility for errors or
omissions.

Calcot Park Golf Club

The First 75 Years

1930 – 2005

Compiled & Written by
John Wheeler

First Published in Great Britain in 2005 by
Calcot Golf Club Limited
Bath Road, Calcot, Reading. RG31 7RN

www.calcotpark.com

ISBN 0 9549148 0 5

Design & Typesetting by Ray Lloyd
Printed and bound in Great Britain

Foreword

This book provides a potted history of the Club as brilliantly compiled and written by John Wheeler, to whom we are greatly indebted. I hope you appreciate reading both the celebrated and not so well-known facts about the Club's past 75 years.

Calcot Park has come a long way since it was founded in 1930. The Club and Course have been witness to an abundance of historical and political change on both the local and global scene and it is testament to its members and to tremendous club spirit that it has stood firm and flourished throughout these times.

I am honoured to write, as your Chairman, during what will hopefully be seen in times to come as an exciting and progressive period in the Club's history. Calcot Park is already proud to have had a lady as President (and a proper Lady at that). With luck it will also survive having a woman chairing the Board of Directors.

Sue Wethey
Chairman 2005

What History?

We are now into the third Millennium and the Golf Club is only 75 years young – so can we have a history? Yes – because history is all that is preserved and remembered of the past. Those of us today that play and own this wonderful piece of land that is Calcot Park Golf Club, should do all we can to preserve it and remember and honour those who created it.

John Wheeler

Contents

Lieut Col J H M Greenly CBE
1st Chairman and founder member
Calcot Golf Club Limited 1930

Calcot Park Estate

PETER VANLORE was born in Holland in 1574 and came to England as a Protestant refugee. He was naturalised, knighted by James I in 1621, built himself a Manor House in Calcot Park and married Jacoba Thibault. Peter died in 1627 and the Manor House then passed to a grand-daughter and her husband, Henry Zinzan.

Frances Kendrick was born on 20th October 1687, the eldest of the four daughters of Sir William & Mary Kendrick of Whitley Manor. Sir William seems to have been a soldier in King James II army, fighting in the Irish War that ended with the Battle of the Boyne in 1691. Sir William died on 31st August 1699 followed by his wife five years later. Frances, a clever and high-spirited girl of eighteen, became a wealthy heiress owning the mansion and grounds of Whitley Park. Frances promptly went to live at Calcot Manor: as Calcot was not mentioned in the Kendrick wills, it seems probable that Whitley Manor was sold in order to purchase Calcot Manor.

Frances was determined to marry but, having no male relative to arrange her marriage, according to conventions of the time, decided to arrange matters for herself. Benjamin Child, a young London lawyer, was invited to a wedding in Reading. He was a handsome man, with debts from extravagant living in London and considered the Reading visit a good opportunity to find himself a country heiress as a wife. The wedding consisted of three or four days of balls, banquets and routs (an archaic term for large parties or social gatherings). During the festivities Frances and Benjamin met and danced. Frances was at once determined to marry him; unfortunately Benjamin thought she had another alliance and danced with other young ladies hoping to find one unattached that he could marry.

Frances had wrongly assumed that it was her obvious wealth that had deterred Benjamin and caused a barrier between them. So she wrote an anonymous letter to him, as if from a man, indicating 'he' had been slighted and challenged Benjamin to a duel. Benjamin, being uncertain

The 'feisty lady,' Frances Kendrick, confronts Benjamin Child in a duel at dawn
Illustration: Courtesy of David Nash

as to why he had been challenged, and by what 'man', arrived at the place for the duel, described as, "...at the entrance to Calcot Park, at the foot of the slope where there is a fountain, an hour after sunrise, and defend yourself as best you may with sword." There, he was confronted by a masked lady who insisted that he either fight her or wed her. He chose marriage.

Frances had already made the wedding arrangements and had a coach waiting to take them to Wargrave where they were married on 28th March 1706. The bride refused to take off her mask until they returned to Calcot Park. Benjamin happily accepted her beauty – and her fortune. This tale is believed to be the inspiration for the fabled *"Ballad of the Berkshire Lady."*

The couple lived together at Calcot Park, raising two daughters. Frances died in 1722 at the age of 35. Benjamin was heartbroken and had her body encased in a lead coffin, which was made to her exact shape and facial features; Frances is said to be interred in a vault of St Mary's in the Butts. There is however no church record in corroboration.

Benjamin became an eccentric recluse selling all of his property, except Prospect Park, to Sir John Blagrave of Southcote. When the new owners arrived to take possession though, Benjamin suddenly found himself unable to leave. He locked himself inside the house and would let no-one in. Eventually the new owners had to resort to tearing the lead from the roof in order to, literally, flush him out. Benjamin did not quite sell all his wife's estates. He retained the woods in Calcot where the two had met for their abortive duel. Thrown out of Calcot, he created a new park here in the woods, and built himself a fine house with a heart-shaped fountain in the garden dedicated to Frances' memory. The most poignant feature, however, was the view. The house had a beautiful prospect looking out over their very meeting place; hence its name, Prospect Park. Benjamin died in 1767 and was buried at St Mary's in the Butts on 11th May that year.

It was Sir John Blagrave who built the present Calcot Park Mansion in 1755, on the site of the original Manor House. Earlier notables of the Blagrave family included another John Blagrave, who died at Southcote Lodge in 1611. He was both an inventor and mathematician who around 1590 produced a revolutionary range-finding instrument for the use of gunners and mapmakers. In his will he made a legacy which provides 20 Nobles (a former British coin having the value of one-third of a pound) to be competed for each year by three maid servants of good character and five years service under one master, one to be selected from each of the three Reading parishes. The conditions required that the maids appear on Good Friday before the Mayor & Aldermen in the Town Hall and there cast lots for the prize.

The most notorious member of the family was lawyer, Daniel Blagrave of Southcote, a Steward of Reading and a Roundhead sympathiser. He was one of the 59 members of the House of Commons who, in January 1649, signed the death warrant of Charles I. On the restoration of the Monarchy Daniel wisely fled to Germany where he died in 1688. Family fortunes did not suffer as a result of his treachery as other kin had supported the Royalists.

The Blagraves were always good landowners, taking an interest in all associated with their estates, and they provided funds for local hospitals and schools. Under the will of John Henry Blagrave, who died on 23rd June 1895, Henry Barry Blagrave inherited the Calcot estate.

The Mansion was subsequently leased to newspaper magnate, Alfred Harmsworth (later Lord Northcliffe) and, on Tuesday 24th April 1900, the very first issue of the *Daily Express* reported on the first 1000 mile motor rally arranged by the Automobile Club and the breakfast stop made at Calcot Park on its first stage from Hyde Park to Bath. This

118 mile journey was completed in a gross time of 13 hours, reminiscent of the morning run to London on the M4.

The estate remained in the Blagrave family until 24th October 1919, when Maurice George Bauer purchased it for the sum of £27,000. The property then comprised of "Mansion House with old deer park, gardens, stud farm, stabling, garage, coachman's house, lodges, outbuildings and cottages held and enjoyed therewith within Calcot Park. Together with two houses known as Park Cottage and Halls and the Post Office and Village Shop, Village Hall and cottages in Calcot Row."

The Estate was later sold to E H Budd who conveyed the property to Calcot Park Golf Club on 28th September 1929.

The Founding

T HE idea of a new golf course on the Calcot Park Estate was initially tested at a public meeting held in the Mayor's Parlour at the Town Hall Reading, on Friday 24th April 1929. *(A copy of the presentation made to the meeting by Colonel Greenly is included in the next Section).*

The favourable response resulted in a group of Reading businessmen meeting one week later at 16 Market Place Reading, in the offices of A G West, to discuss the possible purchase of the Calcot Park Estate and its conversion into a Golf Course. The Group consisted of S G Chamberlain, Col J H M Greenly, Col J F Hawkins, Major C B Krabbé, H W Lydall, A G West and E Duncan Fraser. Further meetings took place at which G W Spencer Hawes and Commander A F G Tracey participated.

Alternative methods of raising the necessary capital to purchase and construct the course were considered. It was anticipated that a figure of £19,500 would be necessary to acquire the estate and another £5,000 to lay out the course by Harris, Franks & Co of Guildford to the design of H S Colt of Colt, Alison & Morrison Ltd.

The Calcot Golf Club Ltd was incorporated and the first meeting of the Directors occurred on 29th July 1929. Leiut Col J H M Greenly was appointed Chairman of the Board with G W Spencer Hawes, E Duncan Fraser, Commander A F G Tracey, Leiut Col J F Hawkins, John Waddell, Major C B Krabbé, S G Chamberlain and H W Lydall elected to the Board. These nine gentlemen can be deemed

Brad at the Pro's Shop, 1930

13

to be the founders of the Calcot Park Golf Club. The first Captain to lead the Club was Major C B Krabbé and Leiut Col Greenly its first President.

Construction using the natural terrain and features of the old deer park, under the guidance of course architect Harry S Colt, took place in 1929. This was a year of drought and several local clubs were experiencing difficulties with their greens and seeking assistance from Suttons, the local seed firm. Good weather may have assisted the construction and in April 1930 it was announced in the local press that the new Calcot Park Golf course was nearing completion and that 9 holes would be available for play in July and the remainder in early autumn.

The official opening of the course took place on Friday 1st August 1930. Press reports of the event stated that the Georgian Mansion had been completely redecorated and adapted as the Clubhouse to provide a main lounge which looks out over terraces and parkland, a luxurious gentlemen's smoking lounge and a ladies' lounge with an attractive colour scheme. The well-appointed dressing rooms were mentioned as being a feature of the amenities provided for the 200 members who so far have been admitted.

Major L M P Sullivan, then Secretary of Southerndown, was appointed the first Secretary of the Club and took up his duties on 5th May 1931. Ernest Bradbeer, also from Southerndown, was appointed as Professional with an annual retainer of £100 plus the West Lodge rent-free. The Green-keeper was to receive £3 per week plus cottage and the Steward and his wife £3 per week in total.

The Clubhouse 1930

Proposed Golf Course, Calcot Park

T HERE follows here a reprint of the Statement made and read out by Leiut Col J H M Greenly, CBE, at a Public Meeting held in the Mayor's Parlour, Town Hall, Reading (by kind permission of His Worship the Mayor) on Friday evening, the 24th May 1929.

"Ladies and Gentlemen...

Although so many of you have taken the trouble to come to this meeting this evening, I feel sure that none of you will wish to be kept here very long. And I will therefore try to be as brief as possible, but I fear that you will have to bear with me for some 20 minutes or so.

I think I may take it that most of you will have read the circular letter that was sent out and also studied the plan of the lay-out of the course and from these you will have obtained a rough idea of the scheme that the Provisional Committee have in view.

Some little time ago the possibility of constructing a Golf Course in Calcot Park occurred to one or two people living in the neighbourhood and in consequence Mr H S Colt, whose name will be well known to you as one of the highest authorities on golf course architecture and construction, was approached in the matter.

He very kindly consented to come over and survey the land and, as a result of his opinion that a first-class course could be constructed, it was decided to form a small Provisional Committee to go further into the matter. I had hoped that Mr Colt would be able to be with us here this evening, but he has been detained on business at Barton-on-Sea and I will therefore read short extracts from his Firm's report before I go further into the details of the scheme.

We have visited this property on several occasions and have got out plans for an 18-hole Golf Course in the Park. The land available is ample for the construction of a full-length 18-hole course. The soil varies to some extent; in parts there is gravel, there is also a large sand pit on the site, and in other parts there is no doubt clay soil. It must be realised, however, that many of the extremely popular courses have been constructed upon even heavier clay than that at Calcot without the benefit of any light soil or sand being present on the property.

The undulations and natural features of the site will undoubtedly help in creating interesting and testing golf, and we have no hesitation in saying that a very attractive course can be made on this property and one which would compare favourably with the best park courses in the country.

The views over the surrounding countryside from the higher portions of the links are very charming and the beautiful lake adds considerably to the attractions of the estate.

Having regard to the fact that on the west side of Reading there is almost a complete dearth – for many miles – of golfing facilities and that in this district there is a large residential population, it certainly appears as if there is a definite want and need for the construction of a golf course, and in our opinion if sufficient money can be provided and if the scheme is handled to the best advantage, (as no doubt will be the case) there should be every prospect of a successful future for a Club at Calcot Park.

Well, ladies and gentlemen, these are Mr Colt's opinions and I feel sure that as a result you will be satisfied from a "golfing point of view" the scheme is a sound one. As soon as the Committee were satisfied on that score they took steps to secure options on the necessary house and land, amounting in all to approximately 200 acres. As regards the house, it was thought from the first that it would lend itself for adaptation as a Clubhouse, and this has been confirmed by Mr Frederick. Ernest Ravenscroft, the well-known architect, who has inspected the premises.

So far so good; I hope from what you have heard you will be convinced that both the house and the land are suitable for the purpose that we have in view. We will now turn to the financial side of the picture in order that you may be perfectly clear in your minds as to what is confronting us. Having gone into the question carefully and having considered it from every point of view, the Provisional Committee are of the opinion that the total cost of the scheme will not exceed £30,000, made up as follows:

```
                                                                £
Purchase of House, Cottages, Buildings and Land  .19,500
Construction of Course . . . . . . . . . . . . . . . . . .6,000
Adaptation and Alteration of Clubhouse (apart
from Bedrooms)  . . . . . . . . . . . . . . . . . . . . . .1,500
Furnishing and Equipping Clubhouse . . . . . . . . . .1,000
Incidental Expenses such as Purchase of Mowers,
Rollers, etc and erection of Small Shop
for the Professional  . . . . . . . . . . . . . . . . . .1,000
Preliminary Expenses, such as Stamp Duty, Printing
Advertising, etc   . . . . . . . . . . . . . . . . . . . .1,000
                                                      £30,000
```

As regards the cost of the house, cottages, buildings and land, the Provisional Committee are advised by one who has had a long and intimate experience of such things in this district, that they are being asked a fair and reasonable figure and you will see that, including the house, cottages and buildings, the price works out at slightly over £97 per acre, which cannot be regarded as excessive for land situated so close to a growing centre such as Reading. That it will increase in value as time goes on cannot be questioned.

Mr Colt's estimate of £6,000 for the construction of the course is naturally only an approximate one and would require to be confirmed by Contractors, but from his long experience on such matters he is satisfied that his figure is a close one. That then is the position.

It should be possible for the sum of £30,000 to bring 'The Calcot Park Golf Course' into being, as a first-class course with a thoroughly suitable, attractive and up-to-date Clubhouse.

Now, how is that sum to be found and, if it can be found, is there a reasonable prospect of the venture paying its way? First, as to the capital needed. Of the £30,000 required we have already been promised £10,000 by a few people resident in the district. We propose to raise a further £10,000 by a mortgage on the property. We are therefore left with £10,000 to find, and it ought not to be an impossible task. It is true that the security would have to rank as a second charge, but on that I would just say this, as I remarked earlier we are proposing to purchase in all about 200 acres of land, of which some 120 acres only would be required for the course, leaving a balance of approximately 80 acres. Of this 80 acres some 30 to 40 would be immediately available as attractive building sites and the Provisional Committee are advised that these should sell within a few years at not less than £300 per acre, which should permit of the larger portion, if not all, of the amount raised on mortgage being paid off.

There is also an extensive kitchen garden of some 2½ acres, which if not required for use by the Club, could be sold or leased. The Clubhouse and course would then become the property of the Subscribers and should represent a sound security. It is proposed that a Company should be registered with a Capital of £10,000 in Ordinary Shares and that an issue should be made of 10,000 4% Debentures in the form of Bonds of £100 each to those persons who have already guaranteed the £10,000 I have mentioned previously. These Bond holders will also receive certain privileges as regards the introduction of playing visitors without green fees.

As regards Subscribers for Ordinary Shares, it is suggested that anyone who may subscribe £50 or more should be entitled to membership at a reduced subscription, and I will deal with this point a little later in my remarks. In the event of a winding up, all Bond holders and Ordinary Shareholders would rank equally after the first charge on the property had been satisfied. Such, briefly, are the suggestions we have to put before you as to the raising of the necessary capital, and I will now deal with the all important question of income and expenditure.

The Provisional Committee have felt from the first that it would be useless embarking on this scheme unless there was a reasonable chance of it paying its way and, by paying its way, I mean not only being able to keep up the course in a manner consistent with its quality as a golf course but also being able to give subscribers an adequate return on the money they may be prepared to invest. For this reason they have given the question of expenses and subscription a great deal of careful consideration and if you will be good enough to bear with me for a short time longer, I will try to place before you the figures that have led them to come to the conclusions which they have arrived at.

Taking the expenses side first, we consider that in order to raise the capital required we must be prepared to pay an average rate of interest of 5% in order to make the proposition a reasonably attractive one, unless, of course, we may be fortunate enough to find some philanthropists who are prepared to help to finance the scheme for the sheer love of the game of golf without looking for a financial return (not an unknown event, ladies and gentlemen, in the history of other golf courses). If, then, we look to pay an average of 5% we shall require £1,000 a year in interest.

In addition to that there comes the cost of the upkeep of the course, Secretary's salary, rates, taxes and insurance of the property, repairs and renewals and printing stationery, etc. and these we estimate will amount to a further £2,000 per annum, making a total for expenses of £3,500 a year.

Now that may, on the face of it, seem to be a large figure, but when it is distributed over an adequate membership there is nothing very formidable in it. If that sum were required to run a second-class golf course with a small Clubhouse, I would agree that it is a considerable sum, but when you consider that the course will be a first-class course, ranking with any of the leading park courses in this country and that you are also going to obtain a Clubhouse of which any course in this country might be proud, then I do not think that one can cavil at the figure. I would ask those who may criticise and say that they do not require a Clubhouse of this type to remember that such a house is a very considerable asset to the Club as an undoubted attraction to that most valuable supporter of all golf courses, the green-fee paying visitor, to say nothing of the week-end golfing member from London and elsewhere whom we hope to be in a position to accommodate and encourage.

But to get back again to figures, the scheme that I am putting before you has been based on a minimum membership of 300 men and 50 ladies. And in this connection I would like to put before you a comparison. You may remember that in the circular letter it was stated that in Mr Colt's view 'The Calcot Park Golf Course' would compare in excellence with such a well-known course as that of Stoke Poges. Now Stoke Poges has a membership of over 600 men and 200 ladies and they only have the town of Slough and the surrounding district to draw upon, whereas here we have the far larger and more important town of Reading and the whole of the increasingly popular residential district in its neighbourhood. It is perfectly true that Stoke Poges possesses a considerable number of London members, but I see no reason why we should not do the same. Reading is a byword of excellence for its train service and the journey there from London takes very little longer than the journey to Slough. As an example, I would mention that one can reach Reading at 10 a.m. by the 9.15 a.m. train from Paddington, whereas the 9.20 a.m. from Paddington reaches Slough at 4 minutes past ten. (Further, I have the authority of Sir Felix Pole, our Chairman tonight, for saying that the Great Western Railway will grant special travelling facilities for those coming from London to play golf.)

I hope you will forgive me for having digressed for a moment from the more prosaic side of figures. I was saying that the scheme had been based on a membership of 300 men and 50 ladies and the question of subscription naturally follows. To this point the Provisional Committee have given a very great deal of thought and they suggest for your consideration that the annual subscription should be 10-guineas for gentlemen and 5-guineas for ladies, subject to the reduced subscriptions which I referred to earlier in my remarks.

In this connection, the Provisional Committee suggest that the subscription of those taking up £100 or more of Ordinary Shares should be 8-guineas per annum and 9-guineas in the case of those acquiring Shares to the value of £50 to £100. In addition, they suggest that any non-playing subscribers of £50 or more should have the privilege of nominating one playing member at the appropriate reduced subscription, subject to the ordinary rules of election of the Club. The Provisional Committee's reasons for arriving at these subscription figures are as follows:

I have told you that the total expenses are estimated at £3,500 per annum. Now, how are we to meet them? In giving you the following figures there is a common factor running through them all, viz. the income to be derived from green fees and this we have placed at £500 per annum. I will not trouble you with our reasons, but they are sound and conservative and they are based on known facts from other courses of various degrees of excellence. If then, we accept that figure let us look at the position from a 10-guinea and 5-guinea point of view.

	£	s	d
We have:			
Expenses	3,500	0	0
Income:			
Subscriptions:			
300 men at 10 guineas	3,150	0	0
50 ladies at 5 guineas	262	10	0
Green Fees	500	0	0
Total:	**£3912**	**10**	**0**

Thus leaving a surplus of income over expenditure after paying an average of 5% on all capital raised, plus the defraying of the annual expenses of running the course of £412 10s. 0d, or £200 10s. 0d if the maximum number of 8-guinea subscriptions became operative. Not too satisfactory a balance it is true but still one that is on the right side and, as to this, I will have a further word to say in a moment.

It may be that even after hearing the reasons I have given you, you will regard the rate of subscription as being on the high side, but I would ask you to remember that the placing of subscriptions at 10 guineas and 5-guineas as against, say 8-guineas and 4-guineas, would almost certainly mean the difference between success and failure, at any rate during the early years of the course and, after all, the difference between 8-guineas and 10-guineas is not very great to the individual provided he is getting value for money, whereas it will make the whole difference to the prospects of the Club.

Before leaving these figures finally I would like to say one word more. I stated that under the 10 and 5-guinea proposal we should be left with a surplus of income over expenditure. That is perfectly true, but I would remind you that during the next four or five years we hope to be in a position to pay off the mortgage on the property or at any rate the greater part of it by the sale of building sites and by so doing reduce the expenses side of the picture by some £500 to £600 per annum. If this becomes an accomplished fact, then the surplus of income over expenditure would present a very different aspect and holders both of Bonds and Ordinary Shares would find themselves in possession of a rapidly increasing asset.

So much then for the question of Income and Expenditure. As regards Entrance Fees, the Provisional Committee are of the opinion that no entrance fee should be charged at present, but they suggest that the Committee of the Club (provided the scheme materialises) should reserve the right to impose one at any time that they may deem desirable.

I can only hope that I have succeeded in putting the position fairly and clearly before you. If, in your opinion, the scheme is worthy of support, then if it receives that support it may be possible, should sufficient members come forward, to reduce the proposed subscriptions; but this is a matter that must lie to some extent in your hands.

I am afraid that I have kept you for an inordinate time despite my intention to be as brief as possible but I have very little more to say, just a few words on the question of Lawn Tennis and Squash Racquets and I have finished.

It is the desire of the Provisional Committee to provide these at the earliest possible opportunity and so soon as the financial position of the Club shall justify them doing so, and I would mention that one hard tennis court by Messrs. Wood is already in existence and this would be immediately available. The Committee also suggest that all original members of the Club, i.e. say, all those joining before the introduction of an entrance fee, should also have full tennis and squash racquet playing facilities for their subscriptions on payment of a small nominal sum for the use of the courts.

And now to conclude; if what I have been instrumental in putting before you appeals to you, I would ask you, on behalf of the Provisional Committee, to be so good as to constitute yourselves into a large propaganda committee and to endeavour to secure for the scheme as wide a publicity and as great a support as possible. Only a short time remains before the options expire and if the scheme is to succeed real enthusiasm from its supporters is necessary. If we are so fortunate as to find in this room any who are prepared to give a lead, then I would ask them either to say so now or to stay behind for a moment at the end of the meeting, and to those who wish to think the matter over, I can only say that any member of the Provisional Committee will be only too ready to hear from them in the near future.

Finally, ladies and gentlemen, I would say that this Meeting must be regarded in the nature of a Preliminary Meeting. There are obviously many details that still remain to be thrashed out but until the Provisional Committee are aware of your wishes in the matter, they did not think it desirable to complicate the position by putting before you a mass of detail.

I would remind you also that the Committee are purely a provisional Committee and that, should the scheme materialise, they will of course retire and the members of the Club would then elect their own Committee to run the management of the Club. And now if anyone wishes to ask any questions, I will endeavour to answer them to the best I am able and I have only to thank you for the patient hearing that you have been good enough to give me."

The following are the names of the Provisional Committee, either of whom will be pleased to give any information to anyone interested in the proposed Golf Course:

S G Chamberlain
Fairleigh, Priest Hill, Caversham

E Duncan Fraser
1 Station Road, Reading

Leiut Col J H. M. Greenly, CBE
Calcot Hill, Calcot, Reading

Spencer Hawes
130 Shinfield Road, Reading

Leiut Col J F Hawkins, OBE, M Inst C E

Major C B Krabbé
Calcot Grange, Calcot, Reading

H W Lydall
Stoneham House, Calcot, Reading.

Sir Felix J C Pole
Calcot Place, Reading

John Waddell, JP
Beenham House, Beenham, Nr Reading

Important Figures from our Past

Leiut Col John Greenly CBE
John Greenly was born in
Herefordshire in 1886. He was
educated at Charterhouse and
Trinity College, Oxford.
Entering the army, and
naturally joining the
Herefordshire Regiment, he
was commissioned in 1909.
He was twice mentioned in
dispatches in the 1914-18 War
and attained the rank of Leiut
Colonel in 1919 being awarded
the CBE in the same year.

Later, as a trained Civil
Engineer, he became
associated with many major
industrial concerns as a Director, Vice Chairman and Chairman. In
1938-39 he was a member of Advisory Panels to the Air Ministry and
the Prime Minister on re-armament. In the 1939-44 conflict he was
involved for the Government in co-ordinating the purchase of supplies
in the United States, Canada and the UK and for these services he was
awarded the KCMG in 1940.

John Greenly was without doubt the driving force behind the
founding of Calcot Park Golf Club. Having moved to Calcot Hill in
1926 he quickly saw the potential of the Estate as a Golf Course. He
was elected Chairman of the Club from its inception until he resigned
in 1939, though he remained a member of the Board until a short time
before his death on 30th December 1951. He was buried at his
birthplace, Titley, in Herefordshire.

Lady Joan Greenly

Lady Greenly was the first Captain of the Ladies in 1931 and was closely associated with the Golf Club particularly during the war years covering on many occasions for the absence of office and even bar staff. Lady Greenly joined the Board following Sir John's death and continued as a Director until December 1958. Lady Greenly was elected President in 1962 and continued in that office until her death in October 1965 whilst holidaying abroad.

F J C (John) Pole

John Pole was Chairman of the Board for almost ten years to January 1960 and through his initiative and under his direction the move to a "Members Club" was achieved.

As a partner in Martin & Pole he assisted the Club in marketing its property assets to advantage. His other business interests included the Evening Post Ltd and the Ramsbury Building Society. John Pole died in October 1967 at the early age of 56 whilst on a business trip to Malta.

Ernest Bradbeer

Ernest Bradbeer was born in 1900 at the village of Berrow, near Burnham in Somerset, the eleventh in a family of fourteen with nine brothers and four sisters. Nine of the brothers later held professional appointments at various clubs. The boys' golfing experience started when they were still at school: tired of being chased off the links course, the local children constructed two courses of their own, the 'short holes' on the village green and 'the long holes' among the many sand hills.

Leaving school just before his thirteenth birthday Ernest began working on the golf links then, at sixteen, he went as assistant to his older brother Charles at Hendon. Charles was obviously a fine golfer for he held the course record at Hendon with two of the great names in golf – Harry Vardon and Ted Ray.

Ernest Bradbeer
Chairman of the Professional Golfers Association 1956

The Bradbeers *(left to right Jimmy, Bob, Ernest & Fred)*
Jimmy was based at Porters Park, Bob at Burnham & Berrow and Fred at Clevedon.

By this time 'The Great War' was on and little golf was being played, so Ernest made an early entry into the army. Whilst serving with the Machine Gun Corps he was badly wounded only four days before the Armistice was signed. The only fortunate outcome was an early demob in 1919 from Hospital in 'Blighty'. In 1923 he won his first professional appointment at Southerndown in South Wales and the following year married Miss Frances Lawford at Finchley.

Five years later, alongside three of his brothers he qualified for the final stages of The Open at Royal St George's, Sandwich, a unique golfing family achievement.

In later years Ernest couldn't remember which of them had scored best, but owned up that it couldn't have been him or he'd have remembered. The Internet now reveals all, the winner that year was Walter Hagen with 292, second was Gene Sarazen on 294 and A R Bradbeer (Bob) shot 312 to finish in the top 25.

The whole of Ernest's life was devoted to golf, seven years at Southerndown but the major part of it – nearly 39 years – at Calcot Park, which he joined as the first Professional in 1930 and of which he was made a Life Member in 1937.

On many occasions during the difficult years for the Club Ernest took over the role of Secretary. In particular during and just after the Second World War, whilst Lady Greenly looked after the administration inside, Ernest additionally supervised what remained of the outside staff and succeeded in keeping the full eighteen holes in play. Ernest, occasionally with son Jeffrey's assistance, mowed the greens and the sheep took care of the fairways. During these years the Clubhouse was run by the family. Ernest and Frances took over the duties of the Steward, and with the help of eldest daughter Sheila and sister-in-law Sue who also catered for the residents in the Mansion. Anyone who remembers the minute food rations of the time will appreciate the problems these ladies had in keeping each person's rations separate and under control. During this time the Bradbeer family moved from the West Lodge into the Mansion.

Brad entered the administrative side of Professional golf in 1935 when he was elected to the Executive Committee of the PGA and remained there until a further period as Club Secretary made commitments which necessitated his resignation. In 1950 Brad was involved in the formation of the Southern Section of the PGA becoming its first Chairman and holding office for three years. Brad was elected Chairman of the PGA in 1957 and re-elected to the position in 1958. It was in that first year that the British team (no Europe then) won the Ryder Cup at Lindrick and Brad was proud to have the famous Cup displayed at Calcot for a few months.

Henry Longhurst and Peter Alliss, although they have graced our TV screens for some decades, are but new boys compared to Brad, for he appeared on television in 1938. In a press interview regarding his retirement he recalled the heat under the lights in the studio at Alexandra Palace on July 7th 1938 when he attended for a

Geoffrey Lydall, with the Ryder Cup at Calcot Park, 1957

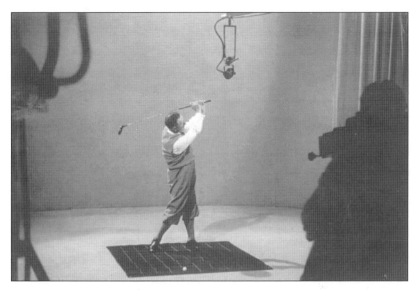

rehearsal of a programme '*A Lesson on Golf*' which was to be transmitted that evening. The programme was considered a success and he was engaged to do a series of eight further programmes; these came to an end when war was approaching.

Ernest was on TV again in 1957, this time as Chairman of the PGA. Alongside the winning of the Ryder Cup there was an unfortunate incident involving one of the players, Harry Weetman, who had taken umbrage at being dropped for one of the matches and made comments regarding the then team Captain, Dai Rees. Brad smoothed things out and avoided the threatened suspension of Weetman.

The second honour bestowed on Brad by his fellow professionals was his election as Captain of the PGA in 1960; this was the year of the Centenary Open Championship played at St Andrews.

Arthur, Brad and Frances at the Pro's Shop in 1960

Brad had more controversy to deal with during this year of office. The tournament professionals were discontented with the arrangements for sponsored events in the golfing calendar, which meant they had to choose between the home circuit and European Championship events. Brad's diplomacy prevented a split in the professional ranks and touring professionals gained places on the Executive Committee.

Brad wrote a weekly golf column in the *"Reading Standard"* for many years reporting on the competitions and social activities at all the clubs in the area. During the winter months, when there was less to report on, his column included articles of golf instruction and short tips for players.

The only regret that Brad had when he retired was that his nephew Arthur would not be taking over from him as the Calcot Park Professional. The Directors of the Club had resolved to offer the Professional's position to Arthur whenever Ernest decided to retire. Sadly the opportunity never came, for Arthur died suddenly in 1968. Arthur had been Brad's Assistant for over 32 years, a loyal, popular,

Presentation at Brad's Retirement Party on 6th August 1968
Stuart Hill, Maurice Ash (Captain), Tom Evans (Secretary) and Jack Kingston (President)
Frances and Ernest Bradbeer

modest and efficient man whose golfing potential had not been exploited. He had been much more than a nephew and his demise brought considerable grief. The Club renamed the existing Mixed Foursomes Competition the 'Arthur Bradbeer' Foursomes as a memorial to him.

Forced by ill health, Brad's retirement came in 1968, and the Club inaugurated a match play competition for the lower handicap players in his honour. Brad died in January 1969 and was buried at St Michael's Church, Tilehurst not too far from the course he loved. Frances remained at Langton Lodge on the Golf Course until her death at the age of 92 in January 1986.

Arthur Bradbeer

Most of the present members who now play in the Mixed Foursomes Competition that bears his name will not have known Arthur; for their

benefit there follows an appreciation, written by Tom Evans shortly after Arthur died on the 27th January 1968.

Having been at Calcot Park Golf Club for 32 years, his untimely death at the age of 48 came at a time when it was hoped he would be restored to good health enabling him to succeed his uncle who after 38 years of service is now not enjoying the best of health.

Arthur will always be remembered for his ever cheerful and polite manner coupled with his patient and skillful teaching. He was a great competitor in professional golf and in 1938 at the age of 18, he qualified at Calcot for the final stages of the *"News of the World"* Match Play Competition. After serving in the Royal Berkshire Regiment during World War II, he quickly regained his golfing prowess and in 1947 was successful with Mrs Baynes in winning the Calcot Professionals & Ladies Foursomes. In 1954 Arthur again qualified at Calcot for the *"News of the World"* Tournament with two wonderful rounds of 69.

Up to the late 1950s, when he retired from playing in National events to concentrate on teaching, Arthur was a great force in the Berks & Bucks Alliance, winning the Assistants Championship no less than six times and the Professionals Championship once.

In 1957 one of Arthur's biggest thrills was no doubt in winning the Professionals and Ladies Foursomes in partnership with Mrs Betty Hallaran. That day they played against Miss Hilda Browne and Bobby Locke who had just previously won The Open Championship and who expressed the view that Arthur that day had played some of the best golf he had ever witnessed.

Later, in 1960, it gave everyone at Calcot the utmost pleasure when, in partnership with Mr Jack Pembroke, he won the 'President's Foursomes' which had that year been inaugurated to mark the opening of the new Clubhouse.

Everyone at Calcot mourns the loss of a great friend and the whole golfing community is sadly the poorer for his passing.

The Thirties

An Advisory Committee was set up in 1930 to deal with the Golf Club administration and in-house matters as opposed to company matters, including the election of members, handicaps and competitions; the committee was formed with the Captain, three bondholders and four ordinary members.

Among the items discussed were:

(1) Monthly competitions were arranged on the first Saturday of each month, medal and bogey alternately. The winners of these monthly competitions were to compete in an annual competition. (Gold Finals).

(2) Permission was given for the Ladies to hold their Medal Competitions on the second Tuesday in each month.

(3) A Local Rule was introduced that, 'a ball may be dropped off either of the two roads crossing the course under penalty of one stroke' and in November, as a temporary measure, that 'a ball may be lifted from the green and cleaned.'

(4) In February 1932 it was permitted to tee-up through the green – rescinded in March.

(5) Annual subscriptions were uplifted for new members joining after December 1st 1930, Men to ten guineas and Ladies to six guineas. Green Fees were set at 3/6d Mondays to Fridays and 5/- on weekends and Bank Holidays.

(6) A one-way system was introduced; entry to the course by the East Lodge and exit by the West Lodge. Speed of cars

was restricted to 10 mph. (No requirement for a man walking in front with a red flag specified.)

(7) In March 1932 it was reported that Captain Figgis had complained of damage to his property in Calcot Row caused by balls hit by golfers. No action was taken. A claim for £5 was also made in June 1936, for damage done by golf balls to a cottage occupied by Mr Tigwell, near the 13th green. Caddies were warned against entering gardens of cottages near the 13th to retrieve golf balls.

Between July 1930 and May 1932 a total of 430 members were accepted into the Golf Club; the initial surge of applications was large but by January 1931 these dwindled to a trickle. Strangely there was almost a straight fifty-fifty split in admittances of Ladies and Men and during that first year the Ladies Section must have had some 200 members – its highest ever. A large number of single Ladies joined as Family Members with their parents and it must be assumed that the latter were expecting the Golf Club to provide an opportunity for their daughters to meet some eligible young men. A considerable number of the new members already belonged to the other Clubs in the area and it is possible that the financial constraints of the thirties accounted for the resignations that followed and caused a 20% drop in income from subscriptions in the second year.

The Advisory Committee was suspended in May 1932. The Board then dealt with all Club matters; aided by a Greens Committee and the Ladies' Committee.

The Company's financial position reached such a low ebb in August 1932 that Major Sullivan's contract as Secretary was terminated and Major Krabbé acted until the appointment of Captain J F R Massy-Westropp in April 1935. Captain Massy-Westropp resigned in July 1936 and Captain E C D de Vitre was appointed and remained as Secretary until July 1938.

Socialising was an essential part of Club life and an Entertainments Committee, on which the Ladies were represented, was set up in November 1938. The committee sought to provide a variety of events in the calendar, although it appears all events had to be sanctioned by the Board and be self-financing. Bridge tables were available in the Lounge from 2pm daily. Club points were fixed at 1/- per 100 for Bridge and Poker 6d ante and 1/- jackpot.

On representation from this committee the Board agreed that the bar should be open to the Ladies on two evenings a week from 5pm. Ladies normally ordered drinks by ringing a bell and were served in their lounge.

A Bridge tournament was held on 10th December 1938, this made a profit of £12 9s 9d. A dance, which raised £25 9s 11d was held on Friday 19th May 1939. This was such a success that it was planned to make the May Dance an annual event, but this was soon foiled by Herr Adolph Hitler, although the Entertainments Committee was reformed in 1946.

On the Course

On Saturday 18th April 1931, in order to advertise the new course in the area, an exhibition match was arranged featuring Charles Whitcombe, the Ryder Cup Team Captain, George Duncan a Ryder Cup player and 1920 Open Champion, A J Young, the Sonning Professional and Ernest Bradbeer. Young had previously gone round the course in 75 against the bogey of 78 so a good match was expected.

In the morning Medal rounds were played; Whitcombe, whose card read:

5 4 6 3 3 5 3 5 5 = **39**   and   4 4 3 2 6 4 4 3 4 = **34**

making a total of 73, headed the four with Duncan one behind. The feature of the morning's play was the eagle by Whitcombe on the bogey five 12th, the result of sinking a 100 yard approach shot. Not surprisingly, with the new greens, the players found putting difficult.

In the afternoon the Ryder Cup pair played the local professionals in a foursomes competition, which they won 2 and 1. Approximate scores for the pairs were 67 and 70. The afternoon started with two threes for Whitcombe to put his side two up; the local pair fought back well and after two halved holes, won the next three.

The visitors won the 8th, and the 9th was halved. Whitcombe won on the 10th with a birdie and the 11th was halved. Young won the 12th but Duncan took the next two; the 15th and 16th were halved and the match ended on the 17th where no one could better a bogey.

A local press commentary on the match compares the styles of

Whitcombe and Duncan and their preference in using different clubs for a similar shot, Whitcombe's 'niblick' versus Duncan's 'mashie' and 'iron' against 'baffy'.

A few weeks later, on the 9th May 1931, Calcot Park hosted its first inter-club match. It was against Sonning Golf Club, and the Clubs were represented by:

Calcot	Sonning
R C Goadby	C H Brickhill
N H Player	S Oades
S C Wells	F J Clyne
S C Allcock	W F Kynaston
Major C B Krabbé	S C Loades
E W Bradley	Capt J F Aston
H R Fosbury	P Blagrave
J H Hay	Gen Phipps-Hornby VC

Calcot won a close match; only two matches failed to reach the 18th green. The singles were won by 4 matches to 3 and the foursomes by 3 matches to 1; an overall 7 against 4 victory. An interesting inclusion in the Sonning team was General Edmund Phipps-Hornby who, as a 23 year-old, won the Victoria Cross in the Boer War.

A 36-hole qualifying round for the *"News of the World"* Match Play Championship was held at the Club in September 1937. The eventual winner, Allan Dailey of Wanstead, posted a new course record of 67 in his two round total of 136. Arthur Bradbeer did a first round 71 but slipped to a second round 76 and failed to qualify. Brad had a first round 81, which finished his chances, but another of the clan, F J Bradbeer, went through as did Max Faulkner the Sonning Assistant. The competition returned to Calcot Park in 1955.

Picture Postcards of the Course

A set of postcards was produced in the 1930s, which showed some of the holes on the course, a selection of which is reproduced here.

The Clubhouse
Certainly imposing, but that roof looks in need of attention.

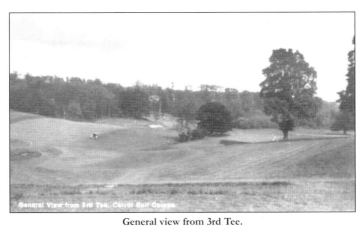

General view from 3rd Tee.
The large tree on the right was behind the 5th Green and was lost in a storm in the '70s.

The position and contours of the bunkers to the left of the 4th green are very different from both the recent modifications and the previous bunkers. The bunker half-way to the green, changed to a grass bunker in the '80s, was clearly not an original feature.

The 4th Hole from the Tee.

The copse now between the 6th and 1st fairways did not exist but the oak alongside the 1st green has changed little. The Lake was then visible but now hidden by the laurel hedge protecting the Practice area. The original four cross-bunker layout is clear to see.

General View from 6th Tee.

If this were an American course in Florida, the 7th hole would be its "signature" hole. It is evident that there has always been a problem with

The 7th Hole

the weed and water lilies in the lake. The trees have grown up well at the rear over the years but what a pity we lost the wonderful Copper Beech.

The 10th looks much the same today except that we have lost a bunker in front of the green and the ditch is now piped across the fairway. These are the six views that we have discovered, there were probably another six so keep your eyes peeled in the antique shops.

The 10th Hole

The War Years, Forties & Fifties

MR STANLEY MANN was appointed Secretary in July 1938, but the Second World War was approaching and Mr Mann was called to the forces in August 1939. The green-keeper, Jackson, was also enlisted and Ernest Bradbeer additionally took over his role. Mrs Greenly undertook the indoor work of the Secretary guided by Col. Krabbé.

Green fees were reduced to 2/6d per round except serving officers who were charged 1/-. Officers' Messes in the area were advised of this reduction.

Indoor and outdoor workers were being drafted to work in munitions factories: this included Kathleen, one of the Bradbeer nieces, making Bren guns in the Prestcold Factory at Theale, and Sheila, the eldest Bradbeer daughter, was nursing at St Thomas' hospital in London's East End.

It was decided to lease the course for grazing, the greens were fenced off and Mr W Cumber of Theale took over the grazing rights for 400 sheep for £75 a year and the arrangement continued into 1942.

The steward left in 1941; Brad and Frances again stepped into the breach, moving into the Mansion with a joint salary of £300 per annum (by 1944 this salary had risen to £450). There were now fears that Brad would be the next to be 'called up'. The indoor staff in December 1943 numbered 10 (excluding Brad & Frances), and the outdoor staff just three. Jeffrey Bradbeer recalls that the hollow short of the road on the 18th was extended across the 12th presumably as a deterrent to gliders landing.

Mrs Rabett was granted honorary membership in recognition of her past work as Ladies' Hon. Secretary.

In 1942 the Secretary reported that the circular saw had been stolen. There were 233 members at August 1942, this included 83 Ladies and the 150 Men members included Military units and Ministry Society Groups.

A regular item for Board discussion was the control of the stock of gin and whisky. An in-house rationing system was adopted which was supposed to limit members to four singles or two doubles per day.

Fears that the Mansion would be requisitioned by the Government were unfounded, although a warning had been given that it was earmarked to house the Headquarters of the Regional Commissioners in the event of the destruction of their existing premises by enemy action; this notice was withdrawn in December 1944.

The War Agriculture Committee in 1942 sought the Club to plough up two fairways. The Club responded that they had no staff or machinery to comply with the order imposed and no further request was made. Reserve stocks of foodstuffs were stored for the Local Defence Committee.

The position of Secretary had been kept open for Mr Mann during the war, but early in 1945 he submitted his resignation, which was accepted. The return of some of the pre-war staff was anticipated, but a permanent Secretary, Steward and green-keeper would be needed. Ernest Bradbeer

One of the original Share Certificates – this one issued to Jack Kingston in 1947.

took over as Secretary in 1945 until Col A G M Sharpe, D.S.O., O.B.E. was appointed in August 1946.

The War was over but not forgotten. The Monteith family presented a Tankard for a competition in memory of their son; the competition was open to all who had served in the forces between 1939 and 1945.

However, the life of the Golf Club returned to a greater degree of normality with the Monthly Medals, Bogeys and major competitions restarting in 1945. The social life of the Clubhouse also returned although food and spirits shortages made catering difficult for the first dance in the Clubhouse on the 23rd March 1946. Subsequent dances and Bridge Drives enabled the Entertainments Committee to donate £100 to the Club for furnishings in the Lounge. In February 1950 the Board attempted to persuade the Entertainment Committee to transfer their funds into the Club General Fund, this was successfully resisted although they agreed to make donations from time to time. The dances continued to be popular and at the one held on 17th April 1953, the 'Max Seeburg Band' provided the music.

In January 1950 the Medal competitions were split into two Divisions; in the first of these medals each Division had 20 entries,

Mr & Mrs Ernest Bradbeer, Mr John Pole, Miss V Harris and Mrs Molly Pole

A Pickard won the 'A' Division with a nett 72 playing off 3 and J L Bates won the 'B' Division with a nett 73 off 18.

Ernest Bradbeer completed 25 years service with the Club in 1955; a dinner was held on 21st October in the Clubhouse to mark the occasion and a presentation was made of an amount nearing £500 raised by subscriptions from members.

Two of the green staff who also completed a similar 25-year service period were Keeley and Bristow; each received from the Board £10 and a letter of appreciation. The membership were however more appreciative of the long service given by Bristow and a benefit was arranged in November 1957 in the form of a White Elephant Competition. This was won by James MacBeth but it is not recorded whether he selected as his prize the cricket bat put in by member P B H May and signed by his fellow Surrey team mates.

1957 also saw Col. Hawkins being made the Club's first Honorary Life Member. The Junior Cup that year was won by Robin Elliott with a net 68; two fifteen year old brothers Terry and Tony Bampton came second and third with net 74 and 75, both off 36.

The "*News of the World*" Match Play qualifying competition returned in 1955 and on that occasion Arthur Bradbeer successfully qualified for the final at Walton Heath. Arthur had two excellent sub-par rounds of 69 and his total of 138 was just two behind the winner. In a field of 100, including four Open Champions and ten Ryder Cup players, this was a great achievement. Neil Coles, the Assistant from Moor Park also qualified. Henry Cotton (Temple) failed to qualify; his first round matched Arthur's 69, but his second round of 76 included his failing to navigate (negotiate) the lake, an incident which is mentioned by David McLaren in the Calcot Park Course Distance Guide.

A New Start

THE Company was in financial difficulties as early as 1931 and gradually ran deeper and deeper into debt. The initial renovation of the Mansion and its furnishing had been almost as costly as the laying out of the course. Problems related to the maintenance, leasing and staffing costs for the Mansion apartments continued to feature in Board discussions through out the thirties, the war years and into the fifties.

By the late fifties considerable sums of money were owing to the Ramsbury Building Society and Barclays Bank; both were threatening to foreclose their loans and drastic action was required to save the Club from extinction. John Pole, Chairman of the day, pioneered the programme to save the Club; this included the sale of Ivy Cottage beside the 13th for £2,000, land to the left of the third fairway for £15,000 and the Mansion for £16,250. The residential side of the Mansion was terminated at the end of March 1959, although services and facilities were retained for golfers.

A condition of the sale of the Mansion was that 'no washing of any description may be hung out of doors', contrary to the ancient custom at the Old Course at St Andrews whereby townswomen had a right to hang washing on the course on Sundays.

It should be appreciated that the Directors of the Club spearheading the restructuring were not major share or debenture holders and John Pole was clearly anticipating opposition from some of those with major holdings at the forthcoming Extraordinary Meeting when, on 8th June 1959, he wrote to fellow Director, George Jones, "My own theme is going to be, all the way through, that never again must overall control of Calcot Park Golf Club be allowed to fall into the hands of a few people." These are words that all present members should be grateful for and remember well.

The Shareholders of the Company approved new Articles of Association at a meeting on 27th June 1959. The Directors then

Chairman, Mr F J C (John) Pole laying the first brick for the Clubhouse in 1960

The new Clubhouse 1960

decided upon an amendment to the rules of the Club, requiring the holding of a minimum of £1 ordinary share of the Company to be a condition of membership; this would not apply to non-playing members or juniors.

The Secretary, L J Foster, resigned in December 1959 to take up a similar appointment at Prestwick. Ernest Bradbeer again temporarily filled the post. The adjourned Annual General Meeting was reconvened on 30th January and a new Board of Directors was elected. Mr T H Evans was appointed as Secretary in February 1960 at a salary of £250.

After the repayment of debentures the Club embarked on building a new Clubhouse, at a cost of £21,340, to the west of the Mansion. The Clubhouse was designed and built by R J Haddick Ltd and, during the construction, a time capsule was inserted into the footings by Mr S J (Jack) Wynn.

The first brick was laid early in 1960 and Lord Brabazon of Tara officially opened the Clubhouse on 1st October 1960. Present at the opening ceremony were the President, Leiut Col J F Hawkins, the Captain, W Parker and the Ladies' Captain, Miss Sally Hughes. At the ceremony it was announced that Honorary Membership had been awarded to Lord Brabazon, Lady Greenly and Mr F J C (John) Pole.

The financial situation was further improved in November 1960 with the sale of the land on the left of the 15th fairway (now known as Broadlands Close). A condition of the sale was that, 'At least one member of each household intending to be demised in the area shall be proposed for membership of Calcot Park Golf Club...'

The present day members seem to be unaware of the debt they owe to those who re-structured the Club in 1959-60. The golf boom was

Lord Brabazon of Tara declares the new Clubhouse open.
The Club President Col J F H Hawkins is seated.

just around the corner, the game was soon to be popularised by television and the charisma of Palmer, Nicklaus, Player and Trevino. Had that restructuring not then taken place I would doubt that we would be enjoying membership at the fees we have today. Imagine what a gold mine the debenture holders would have had today with the Mansion and Golf Course as a leisure complex.

There were obvious winners and losers, the property developers of Fairway Avenue, Broadlands Close and the Mansion were no doubt long term winners, the debenture holders probably losers, but the biggest winners were the then members, and the future members, who became the owners of the Golf Club.

Lord Brabazon of Tara, pictured here with Ernest Bradbeer, in 1960 was one of the major pioneers in the development of the airplane in the British Isles and, indeed, in the world. Elected Captain of the R & A in 1952-53, he got down to a scratch handicap, but he was not a really fine golfer – and he knew it. He enjoyed Roger Wethered's description of him as "the best bad golfer in England".

Finance & Membership

USUALLY the first question anyone asks is, "What's it going to cost me?" Well I can't tell you what your membership is going to cost you in the future but I can show you what it has cost in the past and how the costs of the running of the Club have changed over the last 75 years.

Table 1 summarises the year-by-year income between 1930 and 1959 from Subscriptions and Green Fees, also that from Mansion rents, the Bar and Catering. Alongside is the expenditure of the Club in respect of Salaries, Wages and the upkeep of the course. It demonstrates that the pre-war income from subscriptions and green fees fell well short of the income anticipated from these sources when the Club was formed and was the prime cause of the financial problems in the early years. Also, that by 1959 although the outgoings had kept in line with the Internal Purchasing Power of the Pound Index, (IPPPI) the income certainly had not.

Table 2 similarly covers the period from the 'New Start' to the present time. The Mansion rent of course ceased and the salaries, house wages and course wages are separated. The indices shown suggest that the Income has risen at a much higher rate than the Salaries & Wages payments have and that the 'IPPPI' has risen even more. I will leave it to the economists and accountants amongst you to debate these points and correct me.

Table 3 summarises the Annual Subscriptions paid by members through the past 75 years, the 'IPPPI', only available to 1997/98, again maybe suggests a disproportionate increase in fees.

Table 4 summarises the numbers of persons in the various categories of membership from 1971 through to 1999.

Getting Membership has, since the seventies, been a prolonged process of waiting lists and five day membership, somewhat different to the experience of a couple of junior members from Sonning Golf Club who visited Calcot in 1962 as part of their hunt for a lower priced home in anticipation of a forthcoming marriage. Having played around (sic) on the course they were refreshing themselves in the Clubhouse when they were espied by the ever vigilant Secretary, Tom Evans, on the lookout for potential members and particularly young blood. He immediately offered a joint membership, at a price of 6 guineas each as full juniors; the young man was unsure that his bank balance would stand such a shock withdrawal but, having to impress his fiancée, took

		TABLE 1				
		FINANCIAL ANALYSIS 1930 - 1959				
YEAR	SUBSCRIPTIONS & GREEN FEES		MANSION RENTS, BAR & CATERING	SALARIES, WAGES & UPKEEP OF COURSE		PURCHASING POWER OF THE POUND INDEX
	£	INDEX	£	£	INDEX	
1930-31						100
1931-32	2608	1.0	462	2225	1.0	
1932-33	2057	0.8	1177	2151	1.0	
1933-34	2213	0.8	1913	2075	0.9	
1934-35	2396	0.9	1954	2248	1.0	
1935-36	2038	0.8	1840	2309	1.0	
1936-37	1923	0.7	1729	2345	1.1	
1937-38	2094	0.8	1514	2286	1.0	
1938-39	2259	0.9	2198	2233	1.0	
1939-40	1917	0.7	2155	1778	0.8	
1940-41	1459	0.6	2972	1677	0.8	
1941-42	1288	0.5	3890	1703	0.8	
1942-43	1193	0.5	4230	1772	0.8	
1943-44	1366	0.5	4517	2223	1.0	
1944-45	1556	0.6	4858	2387	1.1	
1945-46	1681	0.6	4490	3102	1.4	160
1946-47	2221	0.9	3604	3089	1.4	
1947-48	2467	0.9	4417	3451	1.6	
1948-49	2778	1.1	3472	3864	1.7	
1949-50	2677	1.0	4554	4175	1.9	
1950-51	2668	1.0	5100	4469	2.0	200
1951-52	2745	1.1	5464	4824	2.2	
1952-53	2702	1.0	5975	4840	2.2	
1953-54	2702	1.0	5722	4898	2.2	
1954-55	2815	1.1	6604	5079	2.3	
1955-56	2955	1.1	6621	5357	2.4	
1956-57	3298	1.3	5866	5131	2.3	
1957-58	3984	1.5	5412	5432	2.4	
1958-59	4150	1.6	4255	5603	2.5	280

THIS TABLE SHOWS THAT THE ACTUAL INCOME FROM SUBSCRIPTIONS AND GREEN FEES FELL CONSIDERABLY SHORT OF THE SUM OF £3,912 ANTICIPATED WHEN THE CLUB WAS FORMED.

a chance. The account fortunately stood the strain for Mr John Morris and his young lady, Miss Diane Chopping.

There was no shortage of names on the waiting list in 1974 when the same John Morris, as Captain, urged that it was necessary to introduce an additional 50+ members from the waiting list as a measure to avoid raising the membership rates to a level to cope with escalating inflation. A number of future Captains, Eric Burbidge, Bill Pocock and present senior members were among those admitted as 5½ or 5 Day Members. Mervyn Greer was another such entry and he was in fact the 1000th new member to join since the restructuring of the Club in 1960; to mark the occasion the Captain, John Morris, presented him with a Tankard. A photograph of the presentation appeared in the local press, but unfortunately the reporter got the names mixed up in the caption, he obviously didn't believe the younger man was the Captain of the Club.

The main criterion for elevation to full membership was in those days 'get your handicap down' and Tom would arrange things when you did. Even in the early days there was controversy over the admittance of members; in 1946 one sponsor was asked to withdraw a particular nomination for six months in order to give an opportunity for the candidate to be introduced to the Board and Club Committee. Later, in 1948, two members of the Board, who were also members of the Club Committee, resigned when the Board admitted a candidate who had not been recommended by the Club Committee.

The present members 'Smart Card', the bar and restaurant payment system, evolved from the system which originated in January 1976 and required members to purchase the equivalent of £25 (Ladies £15) in vouchers which looked very much like Monopoly money – change was given in tiddly-wink counters. Both systems gave the Club an improved cash flow half-way through the year, and the members (as opposed to visitors) get the advantage of a substantial discount on drinks; an even greater advantage of the card is that it is great for clearing the frost off your windscreen on 'Tom Evans' mornings.

The Chancellor of the Exchequer attempted to do his bit for sport in the 1990s and the VAT (Sport, Physical Education and Fund Raising Events) Order 1994 came into effect on 1st April 1994; this ruled that VAT would not be due from members on their subscriptions, back-dated to 1990.

TABLE 2

FINANCIAL ANALYSIS 1960 - 2000

	SUBSCRIPTIONS & GREEN FEES		SALARIES	WAGES HOUSE	WAGES COURSE	TOTAL SALARIES & WAGES	
	£	INDEX	£	£	£	£	INDEX
1959-60	4,124	1.0	471	1,236	1,785	3,492	1.0
1960-61	4,786	1.2	490	1,700	2,255	4,445	1.3
1961-62	5,669	1.4	748	1,796	2,413	4,957	1.4
1962-63	5,830	1.4	880	2,018	2,787	5,685	1.6
1963-64	5,880	1.4	917	2,237	2,788	5,942	1.7
1964-65	7,208	1.7	1,036	2,338	3,847	7,221	2.1
1965-66	7,650	1.9	1,083	2,825	3,892	7,800	2.2
1966-67	10,286	2.5	1,372	3,346	4,481	9,199	2.6
1967-68	11,279	2.7	1,562	3,347	4,923	9,832	2.8
1968-69	11,682	2.8	2,106	3,596	5,577	11,279	3.2
1969-70	14,181	3.4	2,341	3,758	5,721	11,820	3.4
1970-71	14,865	3.6	2,466	5,057	6,758	14,281	4.1
1971-72	16,461	4.0	3,303	5,462	6,825	15,590	4.5
1972-73	21,144	5.1	3,346	6,911	7,104	17,361	5.0
1973-31.7.74	25,714	6.2	3,807	10,474	8,884	23,165	6.6
1974-31.1.75	13,948	3.4	2,029	5,151	4,218	11,398	3.3
1975-76	33,657	8.2	6,050	13,794	10,872	30,716	8.8
1976-77	34,765	8.4	7,607	12380	13,671	33,658	9.6
1977-78	47,347	11.5	8,989	16,731	16,058	41,778	12.0
1978-79	55,619	13.5	11,272	15,644	16,700	43,616	12.5
1979-80	56,738	13.8	11,084	9,585	19,515	40,184	11.5
1980-81	72,174	17.5	9,538	9,956	23,494	42,988	12.3
1981-82	77,507	18.8	13,373	12,826	28,385	54,584	15.6
1982-83	89,935	21.8	13,705	14,633	29,227	57,565	16.5
1983-84	107,927	26.2	14,334	14,007	32,440	60,781	17.4
1984-85	115,285	28.0	15,374	15,884	37,164	68,422	19.6
1985-86	121,499	29.5	19,090	17,939	42,676	79,705	22.8
1986-87	136,208	33.0	18,891	17,383	40,957	77,231	22.1
1987-88	146,959	35.6	20,687	19378	44,969	85,034	24.4
1988-89	161,797	39.2	22,813	21.972	47,739	70,574	20.2
1989-90	178,494	43.3	25,024	23,180	51,627	99,831	28.6
1990-91	205,741	49.9	29,722	29,695	58,732	118,149	33.8
1991-92	244,906	59.4	37,093	42,865	63,120	143,078	41.0
1992-93	297,900	72.2	38,694	46,500	72,688	157,882	45.2
1993-94	321,401	77.9	37,814	49,961	83,312	171,087	49.0
1994-95	334,721	81.2	43,526	89,916	88,083	221,525	63.4
1995-96	351,091	85.1	43,898	47,679	84,850	176,427	50.5
1996-97	371,097	90.0	45,609	58,454	100,109	204,172	58.5
1997-98	412,911	100.1	55,547	67,213	111,204	233,964	67.0
1998-99	399,833	97.0	56,724	71,887	114,783	243,394	69.7
1999-2000	457,942	111.0	56,159	81,804	127,849	265,812	76.1

The "Internal Purchasing Power of the Pound" index through this period was

1960	100	**1990**	1000	**1995**	1200
1970	150	**1993**	1100	**1996**	1200
1980	530	**1994**	1100	**1997**	1200

All Golf Clubs were in a quandary as to whether the considerable amount of money to be returned to them should in turn be passed on to the members who had paid it in the first place. In order to make a refund to each individual member, each member's payments over the period would have to be calculated and individual refunds proportionally assessed. This process would have been expensive administratively and it was subsequently agreed at the 1995 AGM that the Club should retain the full amount of refund £155,000. The consequence was that the irrigation system was completed and £40,000 was paid off the long-term mortgage.

TABLE 3
SUBSCRIPTIONS AND ENTRANCE FEES

DATE	FULL MALE	IPPPI	FULL LADY	FAMILY	5-DAY MALE
December 1930	£10.50		£6.30	£17.85	
1930		100			
1950		200			
August 1956	£12.60		£8.40	£19.95	
January 1958	£14.70		£10.50	£22.20	
1960		280			
September 1961	£16.60		£11.55	£25.20	£10.50
Entrance Fee	£10.50		£7.35	£15.75	£6.30
August 1964	£19.95		£12.60	£29.40	£11.55
Entrance Fee	£10.50		£7.35	£15.75	£6.30
1970		420			
September 1970	£31.50		£21.00	£47.10	£19.00
Entrance Fee	£10.50		£7.35	£15.75	£6.30
August 1972	£40.00		£25.00	£60.00	£24.00
May 1974	£52.80		£34.10	£82.50	£25.30
1977/78	£100.00		£75.00	£165.00	£60.00
1980		1500			
1987/88	£264.00		£217.00		£146.00
1988/89	£278.00		£228.00	£468.00	£176.00
1989/90	£301.00		£247.00	£506.00	£199.00
1990/91	£347.00	2800	£285.00	£582.00	£230.00
1991/92 (1)	£400.00		£347.00	£747.00	£298.00
1992/93	£440.00	3200	£398.00		£328.00
1993/94	£451.00	3200	£451.00		£336.00
1994/95	£495.85	3300	£495.85		£370.13
1995/96 (2)	£443.00	3400	£443.00		£331.00
1996/97	£465.00	3500	£465.00		£348.00
1997/98	£488.00	3700	£488.00		£365.00
1998/99	£522.00		£522.00		£391.00
1999/2000	£600.00		£600.00		£450.00
2000/01	£650.00		£650.00		£485.00
2001/02	£700.00		£700.00		£520.00
2002/03	£730.00		£730.00		£550.00
2003/04	£765.00		£765.00		£575.00
2004/05	£795.00		£795.00		£600.00
Entrance Fee (since 2001)	£1200.00		£1200.00		£1200.00

IPPI –   Internal Purchasing Power of the Pound Index (National Statistics 2000)
(1) –   Family Membership discontinued
(2) –   VAT no longer charged on membership fees

Table 4

MEMBERSHIP 1971 TO 1999

	Full & Family		Other 5 & 5+		Adult Playing	Total Membership	
	Men	Ladies	Men	Ladies		Men	Ladies
1970	Information not shown in A.G.M. documents						
1971	235	86	60	14	395	401	167
1972	235	92	80	15	422	433	172
July 73	235	93	80	15	423	441	176
January 75	245	86	146	9	486	521	167
1976	249	86	135	15	485	518	164
1977	250	82	143	8	483	527	149
1978	250	82	126	8	466	498	141
1979	251	86	143	8	488	531	149
1980	251	86	145	6	488	543	159
1981	250	84	142	7	483	545	161
1982	292	84	88	10	474	528	153
1983	297	83	99	16	495	540	160
1984	298	90	86	15	489	504	155
1985	294	95	104	15	508	517	159
1986	298	92	98	12	500	521	153
1987	300	93	100	17	510	530	160
1988	306	81	100	12	499	529	135
1989	307	87	99	13	506	536	139
1990	306	92	100	11	509	535	142
1991	302	88	100	9	499	531	139
1992	302	88	112	11	513	521	138
1993	300	92	122	12	526	529	143
1994	298	93	142	10	543	568	141
1995	292	89	148	10	539	564	137
1996	297	94	146	10	547	546	143
1997	291	94	166	8	559	543	136
1998	300	96	148	7	551	556	130
1999	306	97	162	5	570	583	134
2000	318	91	159	10	578	586	136

Notes

a. In 1960 the Membership (including non-playing) totalled 370, by 1971 the figure had reached 568 and thirty years later it is 722.

b. Since 1971 the adult playing membership has risen from just under 400 to 578.

c. Male playing quotas have been raised over this period from 310 to 485 mainly to meet budget requirements.

d. The Ladies quota of 100 full + 15 five day has been constant throughout the period.

Land Resources & the Course

IN the years up to 1960 it was necessary to sell off plots on the original estate to finance the continuation of the Club. Surprisingly no safe-guard had been built into the New Articles of Association to ensure that the golf course land was not sold off without the consent of the members. Some attempt to correct this occurred at the 1961 AGM when the Board agreed to a re-look at the articles after the matter was raised by Mr F Horrocks. The following year a special resolution was approved at the AGM that allowed the Directors to sell or lease property of the Company provided this *"did not jeopardise the continued maintenance of the remaining property of the Company as an eighteen-hole golf course, without the approval by Special Resolution of the Company in General Meeting."* At the 1985 AGM, Article 2 was further amended, to read *"The Directors shall not sell, lease or dispose of any land or buildings of the Company without the prior approval by Special Resolution of the Company in General Meeting."*

Although in the 1980s buildings and plots near the West and East entrances were disposed of, the trend has been to acquire ground to protect the boundaries of the course. Curtis' Wood, beyond the 14th green, was the subject of planning applications for development through the 1970s; the Club supported the property owners of Broadlands Close in opposing these applications, which were then rejected in 1980. Subsequently when the woodland came onto the market it was necessary to raise the original offer to £29,000 in order to secure the land against counter offers, the purchase was completed in October 1983.

The trustees responsible for the Greenly land, behind the 6th green and to the left of the 8th fairway, were also seeking planning authority for development. Ten acres of this Greenly land had been purchased by Lady Greenly from the Club in February 1958 for just £100, there were covenants attached which restricted building and applications were opposed. The Club later negotiated the purchase of some 17 acres for

£48,000; this purchase was completed in September 1982. The costs of these two land acquisitions were to some extent offset by the sale of the West Lodge.

The 1930s sepia prints do not show the course in the same glory as the colour photographs of the Millennium Calendar produced by Ray Lloyd but, looking at the originals confirms that although changes have been made, the course remains in essence as it was designed.

My own personal recollections can only cover a third of the 75 years of the course but in that time we have lost a bunker on the left of the first, 100 yards short of the green; the second green has been re-laid once or twice; on the fourth, the large bunker on the hill was grassed over; the tees on the 5th have retreated into the woods, another bunker on the right of the hill on the 9th has gone and the green successfully re-laid. The tee on the 12th has also retreated and on the same hole the bunker on the centre right for the sliced tee shot has thankfully been changed for a more distant one on the left. The 13th is an on-going saga and we will await developments; the 14th green was re-laid with many turf problems to follow, as we had originally when the 15th was re-laid. The hillside bunker short of the 17th has also been grassed over.

In the Spring of 1952, the 11th green was rebuilt by green-keeper Bristow and his assistant, Fred Keeley. The design work was undertaken by C K Cotton and the final product was officially opened by the then Captain, C J B Woodward, on 16th May. Fred retired from the green-staff in January 1977 after 45 years service.

One name that must be mentioned in a history of Calcot Park Golf Club, is that of S J (Jack) Wynn, a member now for well over 50 years. Jack's achievements over the years are well-documented and include those of Club Champion, Captain and President. There is also evidence of the many instances of his generosity to the Club both within the Clubhouse and on the course. The Starter's Hut is an

Longest serving member, S J 'Jack' Wynn

58

The Starter's Hut built and presented by Jack Wynn

excellent example of one of Jack's legacies, being built and presented to the Club in 1984.

Another 'gift' was the original half-way hut in which members of the Ladies Section took great pride in delivering a welcoming array of bacon rolls, sausage rolls, home-made cakes, soups, teas and coffees. Past Captain, Geoffrey Lydall, bequeathed money to the Club which provided funds to build the more sturdier 'Swiss Chalet' type construction we have today. All of the proceeds from the Hut are used for charitable purposes and many thousands of pounds have been raised over the past years. Most notably, in recent years, were the tireless efforts of Helen Cole and her diligent colleagues.

Many of the more recent members are convinced that the pit on the 5th fairway was caused by a 'Bomb', but I am assured by Jeffrey Bradbeer, who lived on the course pre-war, that it was there when he was a lad and he also remembers playing in the egg shaped brick-lined ice-house situated below ground near the 16th tee, and also the open ditch at the bottom of the 16th from which a free drop was obtained – but only if driven into off the tee.

The most devastating change on the course has been the loss of specimen trees over the years. November 1971 brought the first cases of the dreaded Dutch Elm disease; trees on the 6th and more by the 5th green were felled in May 1971 in an attempt to stop the infection spreading, to no avail; then, trees on the 11th and 17th had to be felled. After 30 years there seems no answer to that nasty little beetle and we are resigned to seeing the new growth from the old stumps succumbing again when nearing maturity.

The 'Big Storms' have destroyed many landmark trees, one behind the 5th green, the Copper Beech behind the 7th green and the Lime to the left of the 18th opposite the Clubhouse. Friends of Stan Wicks have replaced the latter and the Club has made great efforts to replace lost and old trees and to generally increase the numbers of trees adjacent to the fairways. More recently, in 2002, yet another severe storm brought a large oak tree crashing down across West Drive onto the corner of the Clubhouse. The building survived, but only from the fact that Sean O'Shea's car had broken its fall. Furthermore, Sean was in the car at the time, on his way home and luckily came to no harm, which is more than could be said for his car. Many people came to his rescue and he assured them that he was perfectly alright, although he admitted later, in the Clubhouse, that perhaps he was rather more shaken than he first thought commenting, "Never, in all my life have I refused so many free drinks!"

An old friend was involved in the early fund-raising to assist in the tree planting, E G (Rocky) Loverock was given permission in 1978 to run a draw through the winter on the "Tom Evans" Sunday each month. The results of 'Rocky's draw are still eagerly awaited, carried on after Rocky's death in 1991 by Roy Culverwell, followed by Spencer Wood and lately, by Brian Cook.

1988 brought blistered hands and aching backs to the too few volunteers who were dragooned into the Lake Project by then Captain, Bill Pocock. The results of their efforts can only be appreciated by those who can remember the muddy overgrown tracks around the lake and compare that with the shrub and daffodil-lined pathways we have today. The stonework bridges are eye-catching features on each side, unfortunately one lady member's electric trolley was too low slung and she complained of 'bottoming out' on the hump.

Another complaint about the 'Humps' caused hilarity at a Board Meeting when John Morris complained that he had lost two exhaust pipes off his sports car due to hitting the 'sleeping policemen' on the driveway. He proceeded to demonstrate, with the Secretary in the car, that the humps could only be negotiated at speed; the experience convinced Tom Evans and the humps were lowered. Ruby Macklin's problem was also resolved.

In 1977, Tony Bampton suggested to the Board that each of the holes should be named; most of the names suggested by Tony were adopted and a new card was introduced with this feature included. Some of the names utilised identified physical features of the course or an adjacent location whilst others commemorated a personality that had

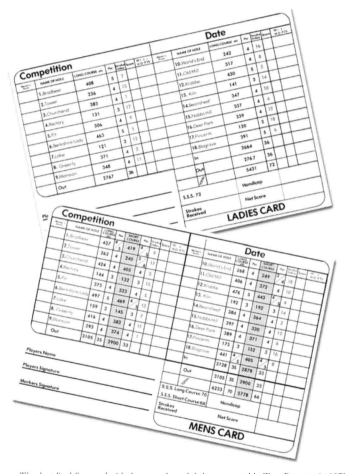

The short-lived Scorecard with the names for each hole as suggested by Tony Bampton in 1977

featured in the Club's past. The use of the new style card was discontinued after only a short time; it was larger than the present card as, in addition to the hole names, advertising was also included but, with separate sections for the Ladies and the Men, there was in fact less room to write in the scores.

The conifer hedge behind the 16th was planted in the late 1980s by a working party of Percy Allen, Sammy Goff and John Leach 'supervised' by Jack Pembroke whilst leaning on his shovel and smoking cigarettes.

The Clubhouse

DESPITE having a building constructed in 1960, the members were considering proposals for alterations as early as 1971. But it wasn't until the Extraordinary General Meeting on 7th August 1985 that the Board were authorised to proceed with an extension to the building. Regrettably, the original estimate of £200,000 could not be met, largely due to structural problems not previously apparent, and a further EGM was called in June 1986 at which the Board sought authority for additional expenditure amounting to £45,000, plus furnishings. The meeting rejected the Board's request. There were only 164 members present at the meeting and proxy voting was a major factor in the defeat.

Married couples continued to lobby for a mixed casual area in the bar, the ladies and the men for improved changing rooms and the administration for more office space. With the sale of land by the East Lodge for £56,666 in November 1990 a 'Redevelopment Fund' was opened. To assist in the financing of the project the members gave approval for the sale of a Plot near the West Lodge, however this sale was not completed until 1998 and then raised £85,000.

The extended Clubhouse 1992

The members' priorities for change were established from some 220 returned questionnaires; alternative schemes were developed and considered by a sub-committee spearheaded by David Wethey and Rodney Taylor. A decision was made, influenced by town planning and financial restrictions, to extend the Clubhouse.

The Development Project was outlined to members at the 1991 AGM and they approved the proposals at an EGM later the same month.

The principal design criteria set were:

1. Areas within the Clubhouse to be multi-functional and be capable of being used as one space for major events
2. Dining Room to be extended
3. New Ladies facilities to be provided
4. Casual Bar to be provided
5. Main Lounge unchanged
6. Conservatory area to be provided between the lounge and the terrace
7. Administration to be transferred to the first floor

Structural work commenced in February 1992, the Members Bar and the Ladies changing rooms were available by June and the whole project was completed within the agreed time schedule of 17 weeks. The total cost was in the order of £450,000.

The Annual Dinner then returned to the Club after travelling to many different venues across the county including the now extinct Great Western Hotel in Reading, Phyllis Court at Henley, the Masonic Centre at Sindlesham and the Calcot Hotel. It was nice to come home and the drinks were better priced.

It is now over 30 years since the air accident in Spain that robbed the Club of two popular members of the house staff. Alejandro Dorrio Mendez and Mercedes Fernandez Serantes (Alex and Chere) were visiting their native Spain and were on an internal flight from Madrid to Corruna when it crashed at Oleiros on 13th August 1973. A Requiem Mass was held at the Church of the English Martyrs in the October and the Club sent a plaque to the families, which was mounted on the headstone of the grave in accordance with local custom.

In the seventies Bill and Doris Tozer were almost furniture fittings at the Club, they were always there behind the bar, diminutive in stature

Praise at the 19th for retiring Steward Bill Tozer & wife Doris
Reliability, Integrity and Loyalty.
Tom Evans (Club Captain), Ged O'Brien (Junior Captain) and John Leach (Chairman) at presentation to Bill
and Doris Tozer, who were retiring after 6½ years service to the Club.

but immense in service, friendliness and good humour. When they retired in 1979, they were granted accommodation for life, and on Boxing Day were presented with a television set and £1500.

Both continued to help out at times for a number of years and Bill's tin of biscuits for the booby prize at the Christmas 'Tom Evans' became an established feature.

President Jack Kingston, Mrs Kingston and Mrs Bradbeer

In 1977 Peter Grugeon, an established Royal photographer, presented to the Club his photograph of the Queen and Prince Philip that is now displayed on the main staircase. Peter died in 1980.

The Jubilee Dinner of 1980, celebrating the Club's Golden Anniversary, was held in a marquee erected in front of the Clubhouse. As part of the Jubilee Celebrations Ken Wildey and Alan Quinlan made attempts to beat the fastest

Norris McWhirter (left) presents Ken Wildey with a Tankard for his efforts for the fastest round of golf

round of golf. The first run was aborted due to problems with the mini-moke but on the next run Ken made a time near the 25 minute mark which did feature in editions of the *"Guinness Book of Records"*. Subsequently there were speedier rounds at other courses although there was some controversy as to the length of course required to qualify for the record.

Prior to the Jubilee Year, around 1977, a competition was held in which members were asked to apply their talents and design a suitable logo for the Club. Mr P R 'Ray' Jones won the competition with his unique, emblematic design of using the initials of Calcot Park Golf Club to form the shape of a golfer swinging a club. His prize for designing the winning logo was four golf lessons from Club Professional at the time, Craig Defoy.

The famous Calcot 'Man', designed by Ray Jones and the Jubilee Medal, bearing the new logo which every competition winner received in 1980

In further celebration of the year, a Jubilee Club Tie was made available to members. The tie was dark blue and incorporated the Calcot 'Man' logo which has been the topic of many a conversation since. The logo also appeared on a Medal which was presented to every competition winner in the Jubilee year.

The Club tie reverted to its original design the following year; the colours of green, representing the fairways, yellow, depicting the summer sunshine and silver being the water of the lake. Its origins have also been the subject of controversy over the years. The tie was adopted by the Club in 1930. Unconfirmed reports say that it was taken from that of Calcot Cricket Club, who, previous to the golf course, were thought to have played their matches on what is now the practice ground between the 9th fairway and East Drive. Even this area is disputed as some would say that the eighteenth fairway would have been more appropriate.

The Millennium Celebrations

NEW Year's Eve 1999 was planned to be a very memorable occasion across the world. So much 'hype' was spread around that many businesses used the opportunity to 'cash in' on such a magnanimous occasion. Thankfully many of them had their fingers burned with the astronomical charges they were asking, with people tending to make their own arrangements rather than be ripped off with paying sky high prices.

The Club's annual New Year's Eve dinner dance was itself put in jeopardy because of perceived problems with staffing. However, it did go ahead and it was a splendid evening's entertainment with Roger Pawsey providing the music to a packed house of partygoers. At the stroke of midnight all and sundry were dancing the hokey-cokey down the eighteenth fairway and were delightfully entertained by a superb display of fireworks by Dick Blything, and his associates. Following on from this, out-going Captain, Phil Hadfield, had also arranged for a 'nearest the pin' competition with entrants hitting golf balls towards a flood-lit eighteenth green – Millennium Captain, Kieran Oatley was honoured with hitting the first golf ball at Calcot Park in the 21st Century. For many, with the intake of alcoholic beverage throughout the evening, they hadn't a clue where the ball was going to finish up and, as some would say, it probably wouldn't have been that much different in broad daylight!

The Millennium year was an extremely busy one for Kieran Oatley, none the least for his instigation of the Millennium Summer Ball. A sumptuously decorated marquee was erected on the fairway in front of the Clubhouse and some 362 members and their guests descended, on a sultry summer evening in July 2000, to enjoy a magnificent banquet along with musical entertainment until the early hours. It was also at Kieran's suggestion that this history of Calcot Park be researched.

During this year, a new stone bridge leading onto the 3rd green was built and paid for from profits derived from the entertainment evenings

The Millennium Bridge leading to the 3rd green

*A 'plethora' of Presidents, Jack Wynn, John Leach and John Easby enjoying
the moment at the Millennium Summer Ball*

during the year. It was named, appropriately, the Millennium Bridge. During the same year, monies were also raised by donations towards a similar stone bridge in memory of past Captain, the gregarious Derek Adey. This was erected the following year over the water hazard between tee and green on the 17th hole.

The plaque on the bridge crossing to the 17th green in memory of Derek Adey

The Millennium Bowl, a four ball better ball competition, commenced in this year; a competition open to every playing member of the Club. Messrs Tim Bunce and Paul Stanton were the inaugural winners. The Married Couples Competition in memory of Bill Parsons was yet another competition in celebration of the Millennium. Looking back to the Club's beginnings, the first ever Club Match was against Sonning Golf Club and to celebrate this new Millennium, it seemed pertinent to arrange a similar match – this time a mixed match was arranged between Calcot Park and Sonning, with Calcot coming through the victorious yet again.

The Veterans (Seniors)

THE first competition for veterans, rather unkindly called the 'Senile Stakes' in the Club records, was held on 28th June 1947. The 'Veterans Trophy' given by Neil MacKay was presented to the winner and is still competed for. The Club Professional is not excluded and 'Brad' was the winner in 1951 and 1958.

On the occasion of the 1952 competition the *Reading Standard's* cartoonist, Fred May, visited Calcot and produced a sketch of characters at the Club participating in this event. W 'Curly' MacLean's winning total that year was 44 points – achieved with the assistance of the age allowance. At that time for every year over the age of 50 an additional half a point was added to the Stableford points actually scored; when the age of 60 was reached the 'pension allowance' was increased to a whole point for each year over the 60 mark. Handicap allowances have been less generous in recent years but winning scores still exceed the 40-point barrier.

In 1979 ex-Reading Town Clerk, George Darlow won the Veterans Trophy for the third time. This record was however beaten in 1995 when Ian Meikle won it for the fourth time.

The Veterans Trophy, the Mark Mundy Trophy and the Seniors Open Competition are all part of the normal Club events within the Veterans Section. The Veterans Section, which is strangely not a long established group, organises other internal events (including matches against the Ladies) open to all male Club members over the age of 50 years. The Section owes its existence to the initiative of Bert Yates, and hard graft by Don Whitby who ran it single-handed as its first Captain, then as Secretary/Treasurer for some 10 years.

When Don retired, Martin Ashton became Treasurer and Bill Kenyon took over as Secretary. At about that time a constitution document was prepared and adopted which provided for the annual election of the Section's Captain. Harry Jackson was the first Captain to be chosen by this process. Bill Kenyon continued in office for seven years until John Rolfe took over in 1995.

The original appeared in the Reading Standard of 20th June 1952

74

Matches are played against other local Clubs, Reading, Henley, Goring, Sonning, East Berks and Newbury in the Veterans Inter-Club League. The League was formed in 1976 largely on the initiative of Ron Stanbrook, a member of the Reading Club, although Bert Yates was also clearing the way forward with the Calcot Park management at about this time.

An informal meeting of Veteran Section representatives was held at Reading Golf Club on the 23rd March 1976 at which a framework was agreed for submission to the management committees of the various Clubs. Alf Gear attended on behalf of Calcot Park but Bert Yates subsequently became the Club representative.

Playing eligibility is restricted in the League matches to veterans over 60 and fully retired but this age limit does not apply to the friendly matches played against Temple, Maidenhead, Basingstoke, Frilford Heath, Castle Royle and Bearwood Lakes.

The Mark Munday Trophy was presented by Mr Mark Munday in 1982 for competition between members of the Veterans Section, it to be awarded to the winner of a newly instituted event – The Veterans Match Play Championship. Mark left the area in 1983 retiring to the south coast returning occasionally in the early 1980s to present his trophy.

In the first year of the competition (1983) 38 veterans entered and the trophy was won by Mr T Walsh who defeated George Hoggett 3 & 1 in the Final. Other members who participated in that first event were Don Whitby, Harry Jackson, Ian Meikle, Sid Cousins and Bill Kenyon. George did win the following year (1984) by defeating Jack Midwood at the 20th hole.

In recent years, with the introduction of 'political correctness' the Veterans have now been renamed 'The Seniors'.

The Ladies Section

THE Captain of the Ladies Section for the first year of the Club was appointed by the Board and, not surprisingly, the wife of the Chairman of the Board was selected to fill the position. There can, however, be no argument that the choice was not the right one for Mrs Joan Greenly was a life-long tower of strength for the Club.

The Ladies have always been responsible for their own organisation and the running of their internal competitions, Medals, Invitations and Inter-Club matches; these responsibilities fall each year on the Ladies' Captain, her supporting committee and the Honorary Secretaries and Honorary Treasurer.

Ladies representation on the Board began as early as 1932 with the election of Miss V Innes Ewing. This lady served for just 9 months before moving abroad; no other lady was elected until Lady Greenly joined the Board following the death of her husband.

In January 1960, with the re-structuring of the Club, two ladies, Mrs J C Jones and Miss V Harris, were elected to the newly formed Board. Miss Sally Hughes also served from 1961 to 1967 and later lady members were Mrs K Male (1962-1967); Mrs H S Wilson (1968-1973); Miss Margaret Perry (1969 & 1978-1983); Mrs Nora Williams (1973-1978 &1983-1989); Mrs M J Wheeler (1987-1990); Mrs H Dyer (1991-1997); Mrs E Pocock (1997-2000). Presently, Mrs Sue Wethey is the Chairman.

Until 1987, Board representation for the ladies had been assured by the local rule that, *"If there were no lady member on the Board, the lady candidate with the highest number of votes would be elected, whether or not a sufficient majority over male candidates had been secured in the election at the Company AGM"*. At this point in time, it was deemed that the rule was in contravention of Company Law and all candidates were then required to stand for election on an equal basis.

The Ladies' Committee and Officers are elected at the Ladies Section Annual General Meeting. In the early years Officers were inclined to remain in position for some extended periods of time;

Mrs Rabett was appointed as the first Honorary Secretary in 1930 and continued through to 1945. Claire Galbraith then took over and continued for nine years resigning only when the workload of also acting as the Club Secretary became too great. Another long serving Secretary was Margaret Dilkes, who acted for eleven years until retiring in 1980. All these ladies were awarded Honorary Life Membership of the Club in recognition of their work for the Ladies Section. These periods of individual long service, whilst giving stability and continuity, prevented new talents; this situation was rectified and limitations were then placed on the number of years that can be continuously served.

Miss Sally Hughes, having completed 50 years as a Club member, was awarded Honorary Membership in 1998 and has the further distinction of having been the youngest Ladies' Captain in the 75 years of the Club and all that, during the year of the re-birth and move from the Mansion in 1960. Sally can also claim to be the longest surviving member of staff, her first job, when leaving school in July 1951, was in the office as general assistant to Secretary, Norman Pickard.

Mrs Edie Poulton (County President), Karen Battiscombe and Claire Galbraith at the Berkshire County Ladies' Match v Eton College at The Berkshire, February 1956

During the period 1939 - 1945, the Ladies were Captained by Mrs Edith Poulton who was later elected as County President. In the years following the war, Claire Galbraith and Karen Battiscombe played for the County and were later honoured by being elected County Presidents; Mrs Galbraith 1963 - 1965 and Mrs Battiscombe 1966 - 1968.

The task of re-building the Ladies Section after the war period commenced at the Annual General Meeting of the Section on 21st July 1945; thirty-two ladies were present.

Mrs Norman Male was elected Ladies' Captain and Claire Galbraith appointed Honorary Secretary. Until such time as the LGU Handicapping System could be resumed, it was agreed to adopt an 'In-Club' handicapping arrangement.

Medals and Bogey Competitions were proposed for the usual Tuesday and also on the 1st and 3rd Sunday in the month. However, in January 1946, the Club Committee dealt a severe blow to their plans and decreed that the Ladies should no longer play competitions at weekends. Despite representations by the Ladies' Captain to the Club Captain and the Secretary, no progress was made other than an agreement that the Ladies' Captain would, in future, be consulted *before* any decision affecting the Ladies was made.

Club matches against Reading, Crowthorne and Goring were sought but only Reading were able to raise teams. These games, home and away, were played in June and July 1946; the home team won on each occasion. In the Autumn, matches against Temple and Newbury were arranged. Temple were defeated twice but the honours were shared against Newbury, again the home sides winning.

At the 1946 AGM, Mrs Male reported that, since the weekend bar on Ladies' Competitions, no Medals or Bogeys had been played due to lack of support on Tuesdays. It was proposed to raise the issue at the Club AGM.

Another kind of bar caused problems in the following year; the Club Secretary advised that Ladies would, in future, be allowed to enter the bar after 6:30pm every evening. The Ladies' Committee wrote to the lady members informing them of this relaxation and suggested that the ladies should not use the stools at the bar but occupy chairs instead. As a result of receiving the letter and obviously objecting to the terms used, Mrs W Wellington Hall, a lady very generous in donating trophies to the Club and the Ladies Section, resigned membership of the Club.

The Ladies, in their endeavours to play competitions at weekends, had 'good news' in January 1947 when Ladies who were unable to play during the week were given permission by the Club to play their monthly competitions on Sundays. But was given the 'bad news' that the LGU Handicapping Manager ruled that monthly competitions could not be played over separate days. This ruling remained in force until March 1958.

In 1949, Calcot members were invited to join with Reading and Sonning members to compete for the Berkeley Monck Teapot and the Club to stage the event for that year; Mrs Fortescue, a Calcot member, was the winner.

The 'Open' meeting at Calcot in 1950 attracted a record entry of 76 which, unfortunately had to be restricted to just 64. A Swedish Touring Team of 14 players competed and, in their number was the Swedish Champion, Miss Butt Karlsson, who was the eventual winner of the 'Wellington Hall' Challenge Tray – the scratch trophy for the event. The Swedish Touring Team who had just previously been defeated by Berkshire Ladies' County Team at The Berkshire, were Captained by Mrs N Runfelt who, as Miss N Gibbons, had been Berkshire Ladies'

Swedish Champion, Butt Karlsson, winner of the Wellington Hall Tray – 6th October 1950

Champion in 1937 and 1938, the first of these Championships being played at Calcot Park.

The golfing lady who reigned supreme in the 1960s and '70s was, without question, Win Henney, winner of thirteen Club Championships, eleven in consecutive years from 1962 to 1972, Berkshire County Champion in 1967, and runner-up in the next two years. From 1960 until 1976, Win played for the Club on over 150 occasions and was a regular for the County between 1961 and 1976. Win was elected County Captain for 1978-80 and County President for 1983-85. Win died in 1996.

In the 1970s, apart from Win, the only Club representative at County level was Annette Mace. In the 1980s, Carol Walker and Alison McLaren joined the County side elite and were followed in 1987 by Sue Ofield. That year, the County Championship was held at Calcot and Alison, Sue, Denise Quinlan, Pauline Lockwood and Lisa Walton all qualified for the match play stage but unfortunately none progressed

Curtis Cup Team 1994
Lisa is third from right in the back row

beyond the second round. Calcot has hosted this Championship on six occasions, the first in 1934 and the most recent in 1998.

Lisa Walton emerged as a force in 1988, losing to Angela Uzielli in the final of the County Championship, but she reversed the result the following year with a five and four victory in the final at The Berkshire. Lisa was a regular County player until 1990, then leaving for America to take up a Sports Scholarship at San José.

Lisa achieved the pinnacle of amateur success in 1994 with selection for the Curtis Cup Team and played at Killarney against the United States. Sadly, the selectors relied too much on the established players and failed to introduce the newcomers until the last day.

Lisa, now Lisa Educate, returned from America in 1996 and an immediate recall to the County Team produced three foursomes and three singles wins in the first three County games. This was an important factor in the County achieving its best ever inter-county match record. But 'Professionalism' beckoned.

Elspeth Cooper entered the County reckoning in 1990, achieving foursomes and singles victories in her initial second team match against

Berkshire County President, Mrs K Battiscombe, presents the Berkshire Championship Trophy for 1967 to Mrs Win Henney (on left) and the Bronze Division award to Mrs C Longden. On the extreme left is Mrs N Tegner, Championship runner up and on the extreme right is Mrs P Driver, runner up in the Bronze Division.

Hampshire. Elspeth also gained the runner-up spot in the 1997 County Championship.

Throughout the last decade, County representation increased with Elspeth, Julie Ballard, Nicola Williams, Hilary Dixon and Chris Green all being selected. Alison McLaren received deserved recognition, being elected County Captain for 1989 and 1990 and County President during 1995-1997.

Ladies' Captain's Day 1955

Presentation by the Ladies' Captain, Miss V Harris, of a silver salver to Mrs Claire Galbraith from the Ladies' Section to mark her retirement as Ladies' Secretary. Winners of the Ladies Section trophies presented that day are also included.

Front Row l to r: Dorrie MacBeth (Victory Cup); Camilla West (Challenge Cup & Ladies' Captain's Silver Prize); Claire Galbraith; Violet Harris, Arkie Burton-Brown (Ladies' Captain's Bronze Prize); Grace Mitchell (Foursomes Cup & Eclectic Cup)

2nd Row: Margaret Perry; Ilene Paddick; Mrs Featherstone; Evelyn Taylor (Bronze Captain); Kay Male

3rd & 4th Row: A N Other; Eleanora Little; Ann Thackray; Madge Horrocks; A N Other; Joan Liddell

Back Row: Gary Burnell; Sally Hughes; Mrs Samuel; Mrs Forster; Mrs Shaw; Clare Hughes; Granny Baynes; Dorothy Harris; Mrs Chadwick

Lisa Walton
Berkshire Ladies' County Champion 1989
Ladies' Club Champion 1986, 1988, 1989, & 1991
Member of the Curtis Cup Team 1994
Honorary Member of Calcot Park Golf Club and of the Berkshire Ladies' Golf Association

Ladies' Captain's Day 1994

Past & Present Ladies' Captains 1994
Back Row: Mary English, Alison McLaren, Sally Hughes, Ruth Winder, Nora Williams, Betty Holtorp, Heather Dyer, Peggy Taylor, Win Henney
Seated: Jill Barker, Kay Smeed, Gwyneth Meikle, Marisa Bass, Eileen Pocock, Diane Morris

Past & Present Ladies' Captains at the Ladies' AGM – 11th November 2000

Standing: Judy Warwick, Eileen Pocock, Heather Dyer, Alison McLaren, Sue Wethey, Peggy Taylor, Margaret Ann Taylor, Jean Burrows, Gwyneth Meikle, Jean Horrocks, Ruth Winder
Seated: Marisa Bass, Jill Barker, Robbie Anderson-Haddick, Sally Hughes, Myrtle Wheeler, Diane Morris

The Ladies & Professionals Foursomes

THE Foursomes Championship for Ladies & Professionals is a unique event that features each year in the Calcot Park calendar. The most notable winning pair were Henry Cotton and his future wife Mme M I E de Moss in the very first event held in 1938. The couple had met in 1930 whilst Henry was in Argentina and married in 1939.

Being the leading English Professional of the day Cotton naturally drew a large number of spectators on the course, but 'Toots' (his pet name for his future wife) insisted that the followers were there to watch

"Toots"

her play. Henry would not have disagreed, for she was a formidable lady and had already warned Henry, "If you put me in the rough I promise I'll hit it back towards the tee. I'm not going to play from the rough. It's enough trouble carrying you around as it is."

He did and she did; in his memoirs he recalls that fortunately the lie was so bad that she had been unable to hit the ball too far and he was able to put the next shot onto the green with his number 2 wood, just two feet from the flag. The comment from Toots was, "That's the way to treat you. You haven't been trying up to now." Henry wrote, "I was mad, but just suffered in silence." Sounds familiar!

By tradition the Club Professional partners the Ladies' Captain. This combination did not achieve success until 1979 when Diane Morris won with Craig Defoy. Craig won again the following year with Lena Watts. Success came to Kim Brake and Mary English in 1986 and to Gwyneth Meikle and Albert McKenzie in 1994.

Craig Defoy and Ladies' Captain, Diane Morris, winners in 1979 receiving the trophy from Ian Richards, Managing Director of the Reading Evening Post, the Tournament Sponsor.

Arthur Bradbeer putting on the 16th, Camilla West with putter and Sally Hughes trolley puller.

The earliest home win fell to assistant Arthur Bradbeer, this was in 1951 with Camilla West and they also came second the following year.

Max Faulkner and his partner failed to beat Match Play Champion Harry Weetman and Miss J Straker in 1952 – not a surprise really as Max had flown from New York to compete and had only arrived at Heathrow on the morning of the competition, pre-jet lagged?.

Bill Shankland and Partner with Miss J Straker and Harry Weetman winners in 1952

Arthur Bradbeer's other win was in 1957 partnering Betty Hallaran who was then Ladies' Captain. Mrs Hallaran was due to play with Ernest Bradbeer, but as he had fallen ill two weeks previously, Arthur stood in. The couple's playing partners on the day were the then Open Champion, Bobby Locke and Miss Hilda Browne.

In 1975 it was the turn of Sally Hughes and Alistair MacDonald (also of the Bradbeer Clan, Ernest's nephew) to pick up the trophy.

Arthur Bradbeer　　　*Ernest Bradbeer*　　　*Bobby Locke*
Mrs Betty Hallaran　　　*Miss Hilda Browne*

Club Captain Ken Thorpe, Ladies' Captain Betty Holtorp, Sally Hughes and Alistair MacDonald

The Professionals who regularly competed in this event were saddened when they arrived at the 'Half-way Hut' in 1986 to discover that Mabel Phillips was no longer dispensing the refreshments, having died earlier in the year. The professionals had over many years been very appreciative of Mabel's services to them and they presented a Trophy to the Ladies Section in her memory; this Trophy is now presented to the overall winner of the Flag competition held in conjunction with an Extra Medal.

The Ladies & Professionals competition also gives an opportunity for 'old boys' to return to the Club they have served as Professional, Assistant or even as junior members; Gary Edmunds, Jonathan Dunn and Mark Squire have all achieved wins, the latter on two recent occasions with his wife, a previous Ladies' Course Record holder and 1982 Club Champion, Sharon, nee Morrissey.

Albert McKenzie & Gwyneth Meikle
Ladies' & Professionals Open Championship Winners 1994

The Berkshire Ladies Golf Association

A NNE Krabbé was the daughter of Col. Krabbé, founder member and the first Captain of Calcot Park Golf Club. Anne represented the Club in inter-club matches as early as 1937 and continued to do so for a short while after her marriage to Tony Duncan in 1950. In 1971, Anne Duncan presented the "Duncan" Trophy to the BLGA for an annual singles match play competition between the Clubs in Berkshire and in that first year Calcot Park won the Trophy, winning against Newbury in the first round and East Berks in the semi-final.

Mrs Stanier, Betty Hallaran, Margaret Dilks, Mabel Phillips and Kay Smeed.
Non-playing Captain Karen Battiscombe in front with the Duncan Trophy

The Final was played on neutral territory, at Reading, against Sonning; the result was a win for Calcot by 3 matches to 2. Mrs Stanier, Kay Smeed and Margaret Dilks were winners but Mabel Phillips lost by 4 and 3 and Betty Hallaran was disqualified for inadvertently playing off the wrong handicap.

Further wins have been hard to come by with a home draw in the early rounds proving critical; in 1975 Nora Williams, Kay Smeed , Joan Jones, Phil Midwood and Mary English won against Newbury at Temple. It was then a long wait until 1986 when, again at Temple, Eileen Pocock, Helen Cole, Ruth Winder, Margaret Saunders and Di Eckersley combined to beat a Sunningdale Ladies team.

Nine years elapsed before the next triumph. Then in 1995, Margaret Ann Taylor, Avril Catto, Eileen Pocock, Vicky Burgess and Sue Wethey beat an East Berks team by 3½ - 1½ at Newbury. Not then such a long wait, for in 1998 Pauline Lambert, Angie Jones, Eileen Pocock, Margaret Rose Taylor and Margaret Saunders won the final against East Berks.

The Inter-club Shield

Competition for this annually presented trophy was started in 1971 between teams of four players; it is a Stableford format with the aggregate of the best three points scores to decide the winning team.

This has not been a successful competition for Calcot Park and only two victories are recorded; in 1979 and 1981. The 1979 event at Maidenhead was won by the team of Alison McLaren, Vera Walker, Carol Walker and Jean Burgess and two years later at Winter Hill Vera Walker, Lena Watts. Helen Cole and Liz Wright were the winning team.

Maybe I'm wrong, a *Reading Standard* press report stated that Calcot Park won this competition in 1960 with Mrs F Thackray, Mrs F Pole, Mrs J Crossland and Mrs G Jones in the team.

The Fourball League

The Four-ball League started in 1975 with teams from Goring, Newbury, Reading and Calcot participating. Sonning and Temple entered in 1976 with East Berks joining in 1977, Maidenhead came in 1990 and Sunningdale Ladies in 1992.

Calcot Park won the first League Title, and also won in 1980, 1982, 1989, 1990, 1991, 1994, 1999, 2000 and 2004. The teams of 1999 and 2000 achieved an outstanding record by winning all of the 16 matches played over the two years; scoring 46 and 48 points respectively out of a possible maximum 56 points.

With the opening of many new golf courses in Berkshire, another division of the League was formed and in 2000 the winners of the two divisions played off to decide an unofficial overall champion – Calcot Park defeated Sand Martins in this play-off.

Team 2000

Back row: Margaret Rose Taylor, Freda Skehel, Alison McLaren, Margaret Ann Taylor, Ruth Winder & Elspeth Cooper
Front row: Chris Green, Julie Ballard, Robbie Anderson-Haddick (Ladies' Captain), Angie Jones & Pauline Lambert

Back row: Pauline Lambert, Julie Ballard, Alison McLaren, Margaret Rose Taylor
Front row: Robbie Anderson-Haddick, Elspeth Cooper and Chris Green

The 20 Section

MOST of the men who start their playing career at Calcot Park are enlisted quickly into the ranks of the 20 Section; here they enjoy a wide range of competitive events and matches against similar Sections in neighbouring Clubs. Some are just passing through to lower handicap ranges but some seem very reluctant to leave the camaraderie of the Section. Indeed, many past Club Captains have graduated from these ranks.

The 20 Section was founded in 1962. Hubert Williams was it's first Captain; he and his wife Nora were great supporters of the Section for many years and donated a number of the trophies now annually competed for. In the 1980s, Tony Lambden took over as honorary secretary and held that office for a magnificent 14 years.

The annual 20 Section Dinner & Cabaret is always well supported by all Club members; a very popular event with the 20 Section Captain

'C' Team Captain, Bob Barnes (left) and Harry Dykes with the 'Barndyke Cup'.
Triumph for the 'C' Team in 2003 & 2004

awarding prizes, usually accompanied by some amusing commentary, to the winners of his Captain's Day competition which is held in the morning on the same day.

In 2003, the 'C' Team versus the 20 Section Challenge was inaugurated with respective Captains of that year, Bob Barnes and Harry Dykes, giving each other so much banter that the teams almost left it to them to contest the match on their own. Much deliberation was made over the naming of the trophy and it seemed appropriate for it to be named somehow after both of the Captains; hence, the 'Barndyke Cup' was officially launched.

In all though, it was a great day for all who played. The 'C' Team triumphed on that inaugural event, winning by just one match.

The Junior Section

I N 1953 the Captain, D V L Craddock, reinstated the Junior Championship into the calendar and the event was won by 17-year-old R L Davis. Over recent years the Junior Section has been watched over by a selection of father figures who followed on in the style set by Nora Williams, the 'Great Aunt' of all the juniors. Nora's aim was to encourage and guide them in the standards and etiquette of the game.

The older generations have not always been so generous in their attitude, particularly when it involves juniors playing at weekends. I recall, back in the '80s, seeing three juniors (one now a professional) eagerly waiting for some senior to take pity on them and give them a game. Off we went after warnings were given as to the etiquette to be followed, particularly the need to let seniors through if they were in danger of holding play up. No problems were encountered on the round but by the time we returned complaints were in of one senior being out with three juniors. The Board decided to amend the rule to make it necessary for each junior to be accompanied by one senior member; of course this restriction no longer applies.

What we can't stand is that they are all so young, hit the ball so far and chip and putt like 'Tiger'. Oh – if only I were! Whatever has been done for our young golfers, or failed to have been done, there has been a remarkable record of achievement by them and many have graduated to the Professional ranks. The support of their families will have been most influential in their success, but the Golf Club and the Members can all take pleasure in their achievements.

Where are they now?

John H Cook
When Brad was approaching retirement he wrote of his pleasure in starting a junior from the beginning, watching his play and swing improve; he added that, "In my old age I will be following the career of young John Cook, my latest protégé." John maintains that Brad was the

finest teacher he ever had. John Cook is now Coach to the England under 18s team and Brad would be proud that his knowledge is being passed on by one of his pupils to yet another generation of golfers.

Mr J V Todd (President of the E G U) presents the English Amateur Championship Trophy to John Cook
PHOTO: GOLF ILLUSTRATED

John joined the Pro ranks in 1979 following a successful amateur career. As a junior playing at both Goring and Calcot he won the Eastern Counties Junior Championship at Sunningdale and the BB&O Junior Championship at Gerrards Cross within a week in 1967.

Still only 19, greater achievements came in 1969, by winning the English Amateur Championship at Royal St George's Sandwich in the July, he became the youngest holder of the title.

The following month John completed a unique double by winning the British Youth's title at Lindrick, his four round score of 289 gave him victory by two shots. His second round of 69 was crucial, there only being one other round in the competition below 70.

John Cook receiving the British Youth's Championship Trophy from Mr L G Winfield (Captain of Lindrick)
PHOTO GOLF ILLUSTRATED

John Cook is now the owner of the Golf Studio at Heathrow Airport and you can follow his Golf Tuition in the "Today's Golfer" magazine.

Mark A G Reeves

Mark joined Calcot as a thirteen year old and was taught by Craig Defoy; within two years he had a handicap of four. One of many junior successes was winning the BB&O under 18s Championship.

Mark joined Kim Brake as an Assistant at Calcot and two years

100

later moved to Badgemore Park as Assistant under another Calcot 'Old Boy' Mark Howell.

Mark then became involved with Peter Alliss in the design and launch of the Dummer Golf Club and stayed there as Director of Golf for three years.

As a consequence of attending the Gary Player Academy of Golf in Germany, Mark was offered the position of Director of Golf at the Royal Jockey Club of Hong Kong. The two championship courses there go under the Chinese name 'Kau Sai Chau'. Within the golf complex there is also a double tiered driving range with 30 bays on each level. The demand for golf is such that the range is fully booked from 7:30am to 10:00pm daily.

Having completed five years Mark's contract was renewed for three more years, he has however acquired a house overlooking the lake at Calcot so we may see him on the course sometime.

Anthony M Ashton

Tony became a member at Calcot in 1972 as a nine year old and stayed until 1982; during this time he won five Junior and two Senior Medals and received a 'Most Improved Golfer' award in 1979.

Tony's professional career began in 1982 as an Assistant at Farnham Golf Club and later at Huntercombe Golf Club under the guidance of John Draycott. In 1990 Tony became the UK National Assistants Champion and Southern Region Match Play Champion.

Tony was appointed Club Professional at The Hampshire Club at Andover in 1993, moved to Leckford Estates Golf Club in 1996 and also encompassed the Head Teaching role at Blackwater Valley Golf Club in 1998 and also South Winchester Golf Club in 1999.

Peter Clark

Peter was 16 in 1976 when he was appointed the first Junior Captain at Calcot, that year he was also Junior Club Champion and Junior Match Play Champion. Entering the Professional ranks he joined Bishopswood Golf Club as an Assistant in 1986, returning to Calcot as Senior Assistant to Albert McKenzie in 1988.

He moved to Germany in 1991 joining Golf Klub Kleinkirchheim in the Carpathian Mountains. From 1995 to 1998 Peter was a teaching professional at the first Golfpark to be opened in Switzerland, at Holzhausern. He is now one of the two teaching professionals at the Golf Club Schloss Goldenberg, still in Switzerland, which is a private members Club with some 580 members and 60 juniors. Peter holds the Course record there.

Robert Walton

Winning the Club Championship in 1993 was the first of the three consecutive Club Championship wins to Robert's credit and in the second of these, in June 1994, he established a new Amateur course record of 65.

Robert's first Club success came as an eleven year old in 1984 when he won his first title as Junior Club Champion. Many other victories at County level followed and in addition to some notable successes at National level there were some unfortunate near misses particularly in 1991.

1987
Calcot Park Junior Club Champion
Rawlings Pied Piper Junior Open

1988
Berkshire Schools Champion
B B & O Under 16 Champion
South East Counties Under 16 Champion
English Schools Final – 3rd and Qualifying for the England Schools Team
South East Counties Foursomes Winning Team

1989
Daily Telegraph Junior Open – Winner

1990
Golf Foundation School's Team – Individual Winner
Daily Telegraph Junior Open – Winner

Daily Express Boys Final – 2nd
B B & O Courage Trophy – 2nd
B B & O Boys Championship – Winner.
English Boys S E Counties Qualifying – Individual low score

1991
South East Boys Championship – Winner at Sunningdale
English Boys Stroke-play Championship for the Carris Trophy – 2nd
at Long Ashton
British Boys Championship – 2nd at Montrose

In 1992 Bob left for a two-year Golf Scholarship at Reno, Nevada State University. Subsequently having passed through the Canadian PGA Qualifying School Bob competed on the Canadian Professional Tour for a short time. Fortunately the call of England's "greens" and pleasant land lured him back home and he joined Calcot Park again in 1998 as Assistant Professional. Bob has now joined Ian Campbell at Ashford Manor Golf Club but, who knows, we may just see him back at Calcot Park in the years to come in a more senior role.

Within the ranks of the Club's Junior members were many extremely competent golfers who went on to become professional golfers in their

The England Boys Team 1991
Back row: Scott Drummond, Lee James, David Hamilton, Robert Walton, Mark Foster, Gary Harris,
Front Row: Simon Crick, Stuart Gage, Lee Westwood, Ian Pyman, Richard Hussey,

own right. Many would say that it was all down the excellent tuition afforded to them by our Club Professionals.

Other names that come to mind are Mark Howell (now Professional at Henley Golf Club), Gary Edmunds (now Professional at Sandford Springs), Jonathan Dunn (now Professional at Badgemore Park), Lee Atkins (now a PGA Teaching Professional based at Newbury Golf Club), Gary Steel (made it as a PGA Touring Pro and is now Managing Director of Oyston Steel Estates, exclusive golf property developers in Puerto Banus on the Costa del Sol); not to mention of course, Bob Forde and Billy Mainwaring.

Harry S Colt – The Colt Cup

HARRY SHAPLAND COLT is arguably the finest golf course architect who ever lived. In addition to Calcot Park, he and his partners created courses at more than 300 Clubs in 24 countries worldwide. Although golf obviously existed before he came along, it always seemed to be a game of straight lines and sharp angles. He softened those lines, introduced curves, and long before the art of pacing courses came into being, created visual challenges to tease and intrigue the golfer. Above all, he was the first to appreciate how golf could be a delightful walk through beautiful vistas.

Many of these Clubs are now regarded as leading golf venues throughout the world. And whilst the venues have preserved their place at the forefront of golf, on an individual basis, Harry S Colt has received little recognition for his work.

In 1994 the Colt Committee was formed with the aim of promoting H S Colt as a leading golf course designer and a major contributor to the heritage of the game of golf. One of the initial decisions was to create an annual tournament, in which members of Colt courses could participate. As such, the Colt Cup was launched at Stoke Park Golf Club in 1994 with the team from Calcot Park, namely David Wethey (Captain), John Taylor (Vice-Captain) and Club Secretary, Alan Bray, being its inaugural winners.

This event has now become one of the more important amateur golf competitions in the world. It has gone from strength to strength with over 200 different Teams competing, including 50 from overseas. The event has now reached four continents, and has gathered much momentum over the past ten years, with more and more Clubs

Harry S Colt, here depicted in an early line drawing

now wishing to participate. It presently also incorporates a challenge match between the reigning Colt Cup holders and the Mackenzie Medallion holders.

Other Colt-designed courses in our area include Goring & Streatley, Sonning, Maidenhead, Stoke Park, Camberley Heath, The Berkshire, Sunningdale and Swinley Forest.

The Palmer Cup & Sutton Cup

THE competition for these two trophies dominates the golfing scene at Calcot Park, Sonning and Reading Golf Clubs over each Easter weekend. The competitions are open to the male members of the three Clubs who are normally entitled to play in competitions, now subject to a maximum handicap of 18.

The Palmer Cup was presented by Walter Palmer of Huntley and Palmer in 1899 to what was then the Reading Golf Club situated off Norcot Road, Tilehurst. This 9-hole Tilehurst based Club did not survive the First World War and its trophies were passed on to the Caversham & South Oxford Club at Emmer Green, which had been founded in 1910. The Sutton Cup was presented by Sutton Seeds to the old Reading Golf Club in 1912.

Both trophies were for many years used by the Caversham & South Oxford Club for domestic competitions but in January 1948 the renamed Reading Club invited Calcot Park and Sonning to take part in competitions for the men at Easter. That year Reading Golf Club hosted both competitions and their members were the victors in both, N Hallsworth in the Palmer Cup and A E Drummond in the Sutton Cup.

Easter 1949 saw Calcot Park as host to both competitions. Reading players were again triumphant, the Good Friday meeting winner was W B Baxter (73 - 2 + 71) and on Easter Monday, B Parminter beat the course, being 3 up.

Calcot Park were again hosts in 1952; Sonning's J C Perkins won the Palmer Cup with 87 - 19 = 68 from Calcot's Fred Thackray who scored 89 - 17 = 72. The Sutton Cup was collected by home player, L A Fisher, he scored 39 points off a handicap of 24. Strangely when played at the other two Clubs the competition was played as a true Bogey.

Calcot Park again hosted both competitions in 1955, but thereafter the cycle changed and the three Clubs now annually host just one of the events in rotation. The Palmer Cup is played for on Good Friday as a Medal and The Sutton Cup on Easter Monday as a Stableford competition.

The "B" Team v the "C" Team

O N the day of the Ladies AGM the men take full possession of the course at 11.00am for the now regular match between the players who have represented the Club in the B Team during the past year and those who have played in the C Team. The Dinner which follows the event is usually rather a boisterous affair but, as the event falls in early November, by tradition the Flanders Poppy must be worn.

The annual match was inaugurated in 1985 by the then 'B' & 'C' Team Captains, Bill Pocock and John Wheeler. Bill has played in every match to date though in recent years he has been relegated to the C's. As a consequence he has been on more winning teams than anyone else

"B"Team 1985

Standing: John Kennedy, Gordon Child, John Leach, Jeff Gulliver, Barry Ofield, Maurice O'Brien, David Reid, David Rixon
Seated: Jim Heyward, Jack Pembroke, Bill Pocock, Tom Ritchie & Tony Bampton
In front (with Oxford Times Cup) Terry Bampton

in the Club, for until 1999, apart from the halved match in the first year, the B team were top dogs. Iain Stapley then became the first C Team Captain to wring out a victory, although John Wheeler claims a moral win for the C's in 1985 as he won his match alongside Norman Carr against Bill in the 1985 halved match.

Photographs of the teams have been taken over the years and many must lie forgotten in albums or drawers. The 'Old' Captains have unearthed photographs of both of their teams of 1985 and 1986. Just four of the early 'B' players retained their places in 2000; they are Maurice O'Brien, David Rixon, John Morris and John Leach.

The "C" Team aged less well, but they started ahead. Only Keith Stewart and Roy Woolford made the 2000 "C" Team. Sammy Goff, Ernie Loverock, Vic Warrant, Jack Butler, Percy Allen and Roy Culverwell sadly no longer play on this sphere but are no doubt making up a four-ball on a greener course. Others no longer play and are very much missed and some of us have moved quietly on to the Green Tees with the Seniors.

"C" Team 1985

Back row left to right:
Percy Allen, Norman Carr, Peter Drewitt, Roy Culverwell, Terry Welshman, Ray Staniford, Bob Stevens and Ernie Loverock.
Seated left to right: Bob Chandler, Sammy Goff, Ted Reynolds, Vic Warrant and A N Other
In the front with the 'Cup', John Wheeler

"B" Team 1986

Back row l to r: Maurice O'Brien, Neil Musselwhite, David Rixon, Ged O'Brien, Chris Denton, David Hopewell, Barry Ofield, John Morris, Jim Heyward, Gordon Child.
Centre: Jack Pembroke, Ray Brown, Bill Pocock, Tommy Ritchie, Terry Bampton
Front row: Ian Graham, Tony Bampton, John Leach, Ed Mcabe

"C" Team 1986

Back row: Peter Drewitt, John Bacon, Ray Staniford, Gordon Kirk, Peter Jay, Ernie Loverock & Keith Stewart.
Seated: Sammy Goff, Ted Reynolds, Roy Culverwell, Vic Warrant & John Warwick
Front row: Jack Butler, Roy Woolford & John Wheeler.

"B" Team 2000

Standing l to r: Terry Bell , Mark Syrad, Gerry Kerr, Pete Honey, John Gatward, Nigel Clark, Colin Dawe, David Wethey, Martin West, Pat McKay, Jeff Turnbull, Tony Coleman, Phil Hadfield, Dick Blything & David Rixon Seated l to r: Maurice O'Brien, Luke Coleman, Dave West (Team Captain), John Leach & Simon Brooker. Kneeling in the Front: Ray Bennett, Paul Keen & John Morris.

"C" Team 2000

Back Row: Vic Hunt, Rodney Taylor, David Bottomley, Phil Parker, Trevor Pembroke, Ron Fuller, Frank Elford, Kieran Oatley, Ralph Smith, Ron Grinham & Steve Andrews. Middle Row: Steve Green, Colin Poole, Keith Stewart, Roy Woolford, Keith Hanson, David Hipkin & Dave Wyeth. Front Row: Keith Goswell, Iain Stapley (Team Captain), Bill Pocock, John Taylor & Chris Bellman

112

Reading & District Inter-Club Golf League

THE League was initially formed in 1967 with the purpose of improving Junior Golf in the area and was as a result of the initiative of Tom Evans (Calcot Park), Peter Boynton (Newbury & Crookham), Jim Bonney (Reading) and Bill Smart (Goring and Streatley).

Starting with just these four golf Clubs, the League was later enlarged with the addition of Henley and Sonning, and in 1987 East Berks also joined. Originally Club's played on a home and away basis each year, but with the inclusion of East Berks it was agreed that Clubs should play against each other once in the spring/early summer and again in late summer/autumn at a neutral venue, six Clubs participate on each occasion; each Club acting as non-playing host on two occasions per year.

In 1998 a second division was formed with Bearwood Lakes, Castle Royle, Sandford Springs, West Berkshire and Windlesham; this division was expanded to seven teams in 1999 with the addition of Sand Martins and Wokefield Park.

In the year 2000 a third division was formed with East Berks 2nd Team, Aspect Park, Badgemore Park, Harleyford and The Lambourne Clubs. Each year the bottom two teams in Division 1 will be relegated to Division 2 and the top two teams in Division 2 will be promoted to Division 1. Similarly the bottom team in Division 2 will be relegated and the top team in Division 3 promoted.

Calcot Park won the League in the first year but has been successful on only two occasions since, in 1981 and 1988.

The Mail on Sunday National Golf Club Classic

JOHN MEIKLE had more than a 'Mark Little' to smile about in 1993, there was Andy Garratt, Ray Bennett and Darren Gatward too. These five took the name of Calcot Park to the headlines of the national press with their achievements in this competition at The Belfry and in Brittany. A crucial factor was the sudden death play-off wins at extra holes on no less than six occasions by Mark Little. It's a wonder he's not known as Lazarus after raising the team from the dead so often, he did make an appropriate appearance at the Christmas pantomime.

In the earlier rounds Calcot had defeated teams from Maidenhead, Flackwell Heath, Evesham and Fernfell. The fifth round was at home against the Coombe Hill team captained by Jimmy Tarbuck. Tarby drew the short straw and had to play Mark, there were no extra holes needed this time, Mark won 3 & 2, Ray Bennett won 2 & 1, Andrew Garratt finished one up and Club Captain, John Meikle got a half; in all, a good 3½ - ½ win. Just one more match before the quarter final at The Belfry, Drayton Park were again hit by Mark in the play-off,

▶ TEE UP — Jimmy Tarbuck (Coombe Hill) with Calcot Park captain John Meikle before their Mail On Sunday National Golf Club Classic tie

Little has last laugh against poor Tarby

The 1993 Team representing in *The Mail on Sunday* National Golf Club Classic
Darren Gatward, Andy Garratt, John Meikle, Mark Little and Ray Bennett

although it took two holes this time. The situation at The Belfry after 9 holes looked bleak, we were trailing 3-1 but in a great fight back the first three matches went to the final hole. Opponents, Bolton, faltered and could only get two halves; Darren had a crucial 2 & 1 win, so it all rested on getting a half in the final match. Mark was one down after the 16th, another play-off looked likely, however he won the 17th with a par to draw level and after his opponent could only make a bogey five at the 18th Mark holed a 7-footer to get the half to send the team to the Finals in France.

The semi-final against Bristol & Clifton was another nail biter Andrew Garratt and Ray Bennett each lost 2 & 1, Darren Gatward won 2 & 1 so again it was down to the Little man. Mark won his match 4 & 3 to put the team all square but then had to play the extra holes again: the 19th was halved and with the opposition driving out of bounds a par was good enough to get through to the Final.

Naturally the final against the Scottish Club Ladybank ended 2 - 2, Andrew Garratt lost by one hole, Darren Gatward had a crushing win by 6 & 5, Ray Bennett went down 4 & 3, so although Mark Little had won his match 5 & 4 it was back down the 19th again for him. With a win already under his belt Mark must have had the edge over his opponent. Although both drove into the fairway of the 356 yard 1st, Paul Stewart, the Ladybank man, was blocked out on the left and could not find the green, his chip left a 12ft putt which he didn't get. Mark's 9 iron to the green covered the flag but his 25ft putt was short – but he got the 5-footer to win and the team became the very first *The Mail on Sunday* National Golf Club Champions.

Supermark!
Mark Little saving the day again at the
Club Pantomime

"Oxford Times" Foursomes

IN the Qualifying round at Calcot, S J Wynn & S Longstaff had been the leading qualifiers with 76 - 4 = 72, however as they had other commitments the next three pairs formed the team to contest the final at Goring & Streatley.

The in-form pairing was that of Claude Davey and Tom Evans; their rounds of 75 and 73 won the Scratch prize and Malcolm Phillips and Bill Parsons won the Handicap prize with two rounds each of net 70½. John Macbeth and Max Bissett came in with rounds of 78½ and 70½ to clinch the Trophy with a team total of 429. The final would be held at the victors Club the following year.

In 1963 two of the winning pairs again qualified for the final, Davey & Evans did not make it and they were replaced by the brothers Derek

Winners of the "Oxford Times" Foursomes played at Goring & Streatley G.C. 1962

M W Phillips.   A W Parsons.   C Davey   T H Evans   J J MacBeth   G M F Bissett

& Alan Adey. The team almost held on to the trophy losing out to Tadmarton Heath by one stroke.

The next time a Calcot Park team had success was in 1978, Tom Evans had a part to play again and as Club Vice Captain he travelled with the players to the final at Frilford Heath. Changes in format meant that the team consisted of only two pairs and strangely again reserves had to be brought in, but this time at the eleventh hour.

The morning round went exceedingly well for the pairing of Jack Pembroke and Sammy Goff they scored a magnificent net 70, but Calcot trailed Newbury as a team by 160 to 161½. So what of those reserves, Bill Pocock and John Wheeler? They were a disaster; they had never seen the course before, the fairways were burnt up in a very hot summer and everything possible went wrong, they scored a net 91½.

Tom gave them a "little talking to" at lunch and in the afternoon round they improved to score 72½, just 19 shots better than the morning, to win the afternoon prize. Jack & Sammy slipped a little in the afternoon but their 83 was enough to give them the best all day prize with a score of 153. The Trophy was won by a clear 13 shots – some recovery. Tom was exceedingly pleased for it meant that the competition would be held at Calcot Park in his year of Captaincy 1979. Would you believe it, Calcot Park won it again. We now no longer compete in this trophy as we are out of the publishing area.

Tom Evans receives the "Oxford Times" Trophy from Deputy Editor Peter Sykes
Jack Pembroke & Sammy Goff   *Bill Pocock & John Wheeler*

Club Competitions

THE Honours Boards displayed in the Clubhouse are a constant reminder of the Presidents, Captains, Ladies' Captains, Champions and Competition Winners of the past that have well benefitted and represented the Club.

Each year our competitions remind us of the Founders of the Club, though anonymously, the benefactors, the Professionals and the Secretaries, and the characters of the past that have bequeathed this plot to us for our passing care.

The premier competition for the better golfers, determining the best scratch golfer over 36 holes medal play, is for the Scratch Cup and the Club Championship. All Champions are noteworthy but special mention must be made of J J MacBeth's four consecutive wins out of a total of six wins mainly in the 1950s.

Bobby Ayres also had six great wins in the '60s and '70s, and the hat tricks for Alan Quinlan and Robert Walton in the '80s and '90s were no less impressive.

Alan would possibly admit that he was fortunate in 1982 that Stuart Scott was engaged in the English Match play Championship at Hoylake. In the first round Stuart defeated Michael Bonallack and was obviously in great form because he lowered the Amateur Course record on his return to Calcot.

J J MacBeth
B B & O Champion 1956
Calcot Park Champion 1953, 54, 55, 56, 58 & 1961
Amateur Course Record Holder 1953
Died 1975 aged 58.

In the years before the war J O H Greenly won the Championship four times and in 1934 was BB&O Amateur Champion – as the latter seems to have passed un-noticed at Calcot one assumes he had a first allegiance to another Club.

Until 1987 the Club Championship and the 'Blagrave Cup' were played for on the same day as part of a 36-hole medal tournament, the former for the best scratch score and the latter for the best handicap score. The "Blagrave Cup" was presented to the Club in August 1930 by Mr H Blagrave, and appropriately was won by his nephew Peter Blagrave in the first year of competition. Peter, playing off 9, scored a net 148. The nature of the competition has meant that no one person has dominated the event, although the same winning names occasionally recur.

Leiut Colonel J H M Greenly presented the 'Founders' Trophy to the Club in March 1931. The format in the first year was to select the 16 players with the best medal scores from a medal round played during the month of June, the Ladies receiving 6 strokes in addition to their LGU handicap.

These selected 16 qualifiers then competed in knock out match play rounds and Miss Bastin, a player of some quality who had played for England and in 1922 had won the French Amateur Open, won the final. This victory stood as the only one by a lady until 2000 when Mrs T Wright achieved success.

Ladies and Men now initially compete in a single qualifying round, with the 16 leading qualifiers going forward to the match play stage. Ladies still receive a handicap adjustment. Successful defence of the trophy has occurred only four times in 75 years.

Mr T E Congdon who was elected to the Board in 1932 and served thereon until his death in 1942 donated the "Congdon Cup" and the Competition dates from 1932. Although handicap allowance is given in the singles match play format, in recent years lower handicap players have dominated the event.

The "Tom Evans" Foursomes was originally known as the A & B Foursomes and was renamed in January 1974, a year before Tom's retirement. Tom introduced this competition format to Newbury & Crookham Golf Club in 1950 during his year as Captain and brought it to Calcot when he became Secretary in 1960. The first A & B Foursomes was held in March 1960 with 48 competitors. Tom and his partner E Locker won the event with a net 68. The winners of that first retitled 'Tom Evans' Foursome in January 1974 were John Leach and R G (Bob) Strickland with 37 points. The individual player with the most 'place points' in any four out of six rounds through the winter wins the overall prize; this was won by professional Albert MacKenzie in 1989/90.

The greatest number of points scored over the 18 holes was probably the 49 achieved by Bobby Ayres and David Reid in March 1973, and the most points scored on a single hole must be the six points scored in February 1972 by Assistant Pro John Draycott and his partner on the eighteenth. At that time the hole was a bogey 5, they were getting a shot and John holed the second shot. They didn't win though; Bert Yates and Colin Graham came in with 42 points. A "Hole in one" on a "Tom Evans" Sunday morning has to be expensive, just ask John *"Don't go home"* Taylor or John Jones to find out the cost. However I think JJ did nicely with the Champers.

Tom Evans originally worked as a dairy farmer at Headley. He had a great interest in sport; apart from golf, horse racing was his passion and he regularly attended meetings at Ascot, Goodwood, York and of course Newbury.

Tom Evans served the Club as Secretary for fifteen years; he was elected an Honorary Member in May 1969 and Captain of the Club in 1979. He died aged 72 on 1st August 1985, the 55th Anniversary of the opening of the Club. At his funeral the Captain and past Captains wore their grey blazers in his honour. He is remembered as a friendly man with many friends.

The link with the Newbury and Crookham Club is also maintained when the winners of the November round at the two Clubs meet in the February event and compete for a pair of pewter tankards; the venue for the play off alternates annually.

The 'Max Bissett' Trophy was instituted originally for competition annually by teams representing Scotland and England, recently they have been joined by a Rest of the World team. Dr G M F (Max) Bissett joined Calcot Park Golf Club in October 1946. In September 1948, his handicap was reduced from 1 to Scratch. 1952 was a big year for Max, he was elected to the Club Committee in January 1952, in May of that year he won the B B & O County Championship at the Berkshire and in the August Medal he returned a gross score of 68 that was at that time a new Amateur Course Record. Max died on 7th April 1982. Years of success for the teams were:

Scotland: 1985, 1989*, 1990*, 1991,   1996, 1997
England: 1986, 1987,   1989*, 1990*, 1994, 1995
Rest of the World: 1992, 1993,   1998
* Match halved

The "Harper Napier" Trophy recalls a tragic episode in the Club, in the space of just 24 hours on 9th March 1980, the Jubilee Year, we suddenly lost the holders of the two major positions in the Club, Stan Harper the Captain, aged only 54, and Ian Napier the Club Secretary. This annual team event commenced in 1981 with a format of any two from four scorers to count at each hole.

Exhibitions, Pro-Ams & Charity Events

CALCOT Park Golf Club and its members has supported good causes and a broad range of charities through direct donations and the support given to Golf Days and through Exhibition Matches and Tournaments over many years.

After World War II, Reading endeavoured to establish links, sporting and cultural, with Holland. As part of a fund raising scheme during an initial visit by the Dutch, an exhibition match was arranged involving Ryder Cup players R A Whitcombe, A H Padgham, Percy Alliss and Arthur Lacey of the Berkshire. The strength of links made were however severely tested when later the same year the Home Office refused entry for an intended larger party of Dutch.

An exhibition match in aid of the Sailors, Soldiers & Airmen's Families Association was held at Calcot in October 1950. Ernest

Back L to R: C Robertson (Hon Treasurer SSAFA Golfing Section), Charlie Ward, Ernest Bradbeer.
Front L to R: Bill Shankland, Fred Daly, Dr Saunders Jones (Captain), Dai Rees, Arthur Bradbeer

Bradbeer was Secretary and was no doubt instrumental in getting Dai Rees, Charlie Ward, Bill Shankland and Fred Daly to take part.

A qualifying competition was held at Calcot in 1973 and again in 1974 to decide the composition of the Great Britain Team to oppose the United States in the Club Professional version of the Ryder Cup being sponsored by McGregor. The Winner of the 1974 competition was W B (Wild Bill) Murray who scored a 5 under par 275 for the four rounds. With eight other qualifiers he travelled, in October, to play at Pinehurst Golf Club. Geoff Norton the Calcot Professional did not make the squad.

A blank date in the European Professional Tour calendar meant that the leading tour golfers arrived in force in May 1977 for the ATS Pro-Am. A young Seve Ballesteros, even then suffering back problems, was followed by a gallery of members' daughters who until that time had shown no interest in the sport. Sandy Lyle, then the holder of the English Amateur title won the amateur scratch prize, but Craig Defoy's score of 71 was not good enough to beat Brian Hugget and Malcolm Foster who both returned 69s. Seves's brother Manuel led the winning team, which included TV personality Kenny Lynch.

Some who watched that day will recall the play of Australian star Jack Newton who tragically lost an arm in a plane accident a few years later. Newton, playing with John Davies an international amateur, enquired from Davies as to, "what was the club for the green?" The suggested 7 iron pitched straight into the firs at the back of the green. Newton's comments were to say the least colourful, probably including a spattering of 'strine'.

Pro-Ams were organised by the Club in April 1981 and 1982, the latter in association with "The Rotary Club of Reading Abbey" in aid of the "Sports Aid Foundation" and other Rotary charities. Three professionals tied for the lead in the 1981 event, they were Bernard Gallacher, Guy Hunt and David Butler all on 70. Craig Defoy our Pro at that time had a rare bad day and returned a 77. A trio of amateurs including members Willie Little and Alan Quinlan helped Pip Elson to the Team prize. Reading member David Brown holed in one at the 13th.

. The introduction of Sporting and TV personalities raised the status of the event in 1982; Bobby Moore, Gareth Edwards, David Lloyd, Chris Ralston and Jimmy Tarbuck participated. One of the senior professionals of the tour failed to arrive for his tee off time; his team waited patiently and were eventually rewarded as they saw Neil Coles – now at the end of the field – shoot a par 70 leading score. The members of the Competition Committee were lenient and didn't penalise Neil for his 100-minute late start. Bernard Gallacher and Malcolm Gregson who were already in with 71s may not have felt so charitable in their equal second spot. The Team prize went to Eamonn Darcy's four, which included Calcot Park's Bill Pocock.

The LPGA Tour arrived in September 1988 together with showbiz stars, bringing glamour and razzmatazz, for the Variety Club Celebrity Classic. The tournament was scheduled as a four-day event, but torrential rain, which fell overnight and on the Thursday morning, caused the cancellation of the first round. Great efforts were made by the green-keepers to get the course playable and it was possible to organise a stop-gap 18 hole competition, starting late morning with four-ball teams consisting of three amateurs and one Lady professional. The weather relented for the next three days and a successful event of 54 holes resulted. Previous British Ladies Open Champion Alison Nicholas won the event by 4 shots from last round opponent Dale Reid,

Bernard Gallacher at the Captain's Dinner

Mike Saunders' Dinner, in November 2004, was honoured to have past Ryder Cup Captain, Bernard Gallacher, OBE as guest speaker.

Bernard is pictured here in the centre along with, on the left, newly elected President, John Morris and 2005 Captain, Gordon McLaren and, on the right, Mike Saunders and past President, John Leach.

Mickey Rooney and Jimmy Tarbuck partnered them in the final round.

The following year, 1989, the event returned to Calcot Park; the participation of Laura Davies brought added interest and larger numbers of spectators on the final days. The competition was however won by Australian Corinne Dibnah who picked up a cheque for £6,500. The final year for the event at Calcot was 1990; play was again over 72 holes from 30th August to 2nd September. Alison Nicholas repeated her win of 1988 and for her 13 under par total received £7,800. Laura Davies was some way back in the field as was the previous year's winner.

Presidents of the Club

2005 –	J S Morris
2000 – 2004	J R Leach
1995 – 1999	T J Easby
1989 – 1994	S J Wynn
1975 – 1988	J A C Kingston
1966 – 1974	D R D Saunders-Jones
1962 – 1965	Lady J Greenly
1959 – 1961	Leiut. Col J F Hawkins
1932 – 1958	Sir J H M Greenly

Chairmen of the Club

2002 -	Mrs Sue Wethey
2000 - 2001	Mr J C Meikle
1999	Mr C K Dawe
1996 - 1999	Mr R J Taylor
1994 - 1995	Mr R Webb
1992 - 1993	Mr J D Wethey
1991	Mr D J Rixon
1987 - 1991	Mr T J Easby
1986	Mr J R Leach
1985	Mr G Cryle
1981 - 1984	Mr T J Easby
1978 - 1980	Mr J R Leach
1976 - 1977	Mr G C Jones
1972 - 1975	Mr F G Henney
1971	Mr J L Bates
1970	Mr B S Hill
1967 - 1969	Mr J A C Kingston
1964 - 1967	Mr S J Wynn
1962 - 1964	Mr G C Jones
1960 - 1962	Mr L A W Spratt
1950 - 1960	Mr F J C Pole
1948 - 1950	Leiut Col J H M Greenly C.B.E
1948	Major C B Krabbé O.B.E
1947 - 1948	D V L Craddock
1939 - 1947	Major C B Krabbé O.B.E
1935 - 1939	Leiut Col J H M Greenly C.B.E
1932 - 1935	G Vernon Parker
1929 - 1932	Leiut Col J H M Greenly C.B.E

Captains of the Club

	Captain		Captain
2005	G N McLaren		
2004	M B Saunders	2003	R Hulse
2002	G F Hughes	2001	R J Sully
2000	K K R Oatley	1999	P Hadfield
1998	C K Dawe	1997	R H F Taylor
1996	E C Burbidge	1995	J R Taylor
1994	J D Wethey	1993	J C Meikle
1992	R Webb	1991	G E J Child
1990	M A O'Brien	1989	D J Rixon
1988	W Pocock	1987	N Ross
1986	J Casey	1985	A Hornall
1984	G Cryle	1983	J F Connelly
1982	B Yates	1981	E V Cox
1980	S J Harper / J H Easby	1979	T H Evans
1978	D N Adey	1977	J R Leach
1976	T Bucknell	1975	K H Thorpe
1974	J S Morris	1973	W F J Cromwell
1972	A W Gear	1971	A W Parsons
1970	F G Henney	1969	E E Locker
1968	M L Ash	1967	S J Wynn
1966	A B Dilks	1965	J L Bates
1964	C Davey	1963	G Underwood
1962	D R Murdoch	1961	G C Jones
1960	W Parker	1959	N E Padwick
1958	B S Hill	1957	J A C Kingston
1956	S H Horrocks	1955	W G Bryan / F J C Pole
1954	L A W Spratt	1953	R W Fortescue
1952	C J B Woodward	1951	J L West
1950	D Saunders-Jones	1949	G H Lydall
1948	H R Fosbery	1947	D V L Craddock
1946	D V L Craddock	1945	J F Hawkins
1940-44	J F Hawkins	1939	C W Mole
1938	R W Wells	1937	D Saunders-Jones
1936	C B Krabbé	1935	W W Hall
1934	J V R Nelder	1933	L C W Cane
1932	L C W Cane	1931	C B Krabbé

Ladies' Captains of the Club

	Captain			Captain
2005	Mrs M R Taylor			
2004	Mrs J Humphreys	2003		Mrs M Bower
2002	Mrs M C Campbell	2001		Mrs D H Macdonald
2000	Mrs J M Anderson-Haddick	1999		Mrs J D Wethey
1998	Mrs J Warwick	1997		Mrs L D Huckstepp
1996	Mrs M Saunders	1995		Mrs M A Taylor
1994	Mrs G M Meikle	1993		Mrs R L Bass
1992	Mrs R J McLaren	1991		Mrs D Adey
1990	Mrs W K H Dyer	1989		Mrs D W Cole
1988	Mrs J R Taylor	1987		Mrs J Wheeler
1986	Mrs C English	1985		Mrs W Pocock
1984	Mrs H Wild	1983		Mrs S H Horrocks
1982	Mrs G A Burrows	1981		Mrs J H Winder
1980	Mrs G E Watts	1979		Mrs J S Morris
1978	Miss J Barker	1977		Mrs K Smeed
1976	Mrs A W Parsons	1975		Mrs B Holtorp
1974	Mrs E A Tarrier	1973		Mrs B S Hill
1972	Mrs J Midwood	1971		Mrs C R Battiscombe
1970	Miss G Mitchell	1969		Mrs A B Dilks
1968	Mrs H S Wilson	1967		Miss M J Perry
1966	Mrs E J Castello	1965		Mrs F G Henny
1964	Mrs H Williams	1963		Mrs J J MacBeth
1962	Mrs A H Little	1961		Mrs J N Crossland
1960	Miss S Hughes	1959		Mrs G C Jones
1958	Mrs D D S Tullis	1957		Mrs E Hallaran
1956	Mrs R G Fetherstonehaugh	1955		Miss V M Harris
1954	Mrs D V L Craddock	1953		Mrs D V L Craddock
1952	Mrs G Burton-Brown	1951		Mrs G Ap Gwilym Jones
1950	Mrs J L West	1949		Mrs F J C Pole
1948	Mrs F R Thackray	1947		Mrs C B Krabbé
1946	Mrs N P Male	1939-45		Mrs F Poulton
1938	Mrs J Dunlop	1937		Mrs N Hill
1936	Mrs C B Krabbé	1935		Mrs L C W Cane
1934	Mrs L C W Cane	1933		Mrs C E Watkins
1932	Mrs C E Watkins	1931		Lady J H M Greenly

Calcot Park Golf Club Professionals

C ALCOT Park Golf Club has been extremely fortunate in its choice of Professionals over the past 75 years. Ernest Bradbeer was indeed a major player and more is said about Ernest throughout this book. Craig Defoy, now at Coombe Hill Golf Club, still holds the course record of 63, using the type of skills that brought him 4th place in the Open at Royal Birkdale behind Tony Jacklin in 1971.

Kim Brake followed on from Craig with such first class teaching abilities that put our junior members at the forefront of golf in the Thames Valley. Kim moved on to Newbury and after 14 years at Sandford Springs Golf Club, Kim was welcomed back to Calcot Park, in 2003, this time as General Manager.

Albert McKenzie, another good teaching Professional, took over the helm after Kim's departure. He is now at that great West Country Club, Saunton Sands.

Ian Campbell, son of past Chelsea Football Club manager, Bobby Campbell, enjoyed nearly seven years as Head Professional before moving on to Ashford Manor Golf Club in Middlesex.

Mark Grieve, a former Tour Player, joins us as we enter our 75th year.. Success at Professional level was in winning the Henry Cooper Classic in 1983 at La Manga Club Spain.

Name	Period
Ernest Bradbeer	May 1930 to May 1968
David Franklin	June 1968 to April 1972
Geoff Norton	May 1972 to December 1976
Craig Defoy	February 1977 to May 1981
Kim Brake	May 1981 to June 1988
Albert McKenzie	July 1988 to December 1997
Ian Campbell	January 1998 to November 2004
Mark Grieve	December 2004

Secretaries to Calcot Park Golf Club

Name	Period
Mr Kim Brake	April 2003
Mr John Cox	November 1998 to April 2003
Mr Eric Burbidge – Acting	June 1998 to November 1998
Mr Tim Harris	February 1997 to June 1998
Mr Alan Bray	March 1991 to February 1997
Mr Stuart Chisholm	August 1981 to February 1991
Mr J W Weir	July1980 to July 1981
Mrs Y M Smith – Acting	April 1980 to June 1980
Mr Ian Napier	July 1977 to March 1980
Mr Tom H Evans	September 1976 to July 1977
Mr E R Illingworth	April 1975 to August 1976
Mr Tom H Evans	February 1960 to March 1975
Mr S Foster	November 1957 to December 1959
Mrs Galbraith & Mr Ernest Bradbeer	February 1954 to October 1957
Mr Norman Pickard	May 1951 to January 1954
Mr Ernest Bradbeer	May 1950 to May 1951
Mr J A Farrar	January 1950 to April 1950
Col A G M Sharpe D.S.O., O.B.E.	August 1946 to November 1949
Lady Joan Greenly undertook the indoor elements of the secretarial duties under the direction of Major Krabbé. Mr Ernest Bradbeer supervised course matters.	Sept 1939 to August 1946
Mr Stanley Mann	July 1938 to August 1939 (H M Forces)
Capt E C D de Vitre	January 1937 to July 1938
Capt J F R Massy-Westropp	April 1935 to December 1936
Major C B Krabbé – Acting Hon Sec	October 1932 to April 1935
Major L M P Sullivan O.B.E.	5th May 1931 to October 1932

Calcot Park Course Records

Men's Amateur		Ladies Amateur		Professional	
W H T Hope 1st Oct 1932	74				
J O H Greenly 16th June 1934	74				
J O H Greenly 6th Oct 1934	72				
R Fortescue 28th Oct 1934	71				
J O H Greenly 5th June 1937	70				
C W Mole 10th July 1937	67				
				A M Dailey 67	
G M F Bissett August 1952	68*	Mrs W Henney August 1963	74		
J J Macbeth July 1953	65	Miss S Morrissey June 1982	73		
S Scott R Walton M A Forde	66 * 66* 66*	Miss C Walker September 1982	71		
Robert Walton 19th June 1994	**65**	**Lisa Walton** 23rd July 1992	**69**	**Craig Defoy** 28th Aug 1983	**63**

* Course changes

135

Ernest Bradbeer

J UST before he retired from Calcot Park, in 1968, Ernest wrote in the *"Evening Post"* the following account of his life and experiences as a Club Professional:

Somerset's Burnham and Berrow Golf Club, as it has always been known, is one of the finest links in the West Country (I would say the very best). Many hundreds of times I have caddied on them at a remuneration of ninepence (4½p) per round. This was the background of my childhood days.

I was born in the little village of Berrow, which adjoins Burnham, the 11th child in a huge family of 14, ten boys and four girls. Nine of us later held professional appointments at various Clubs, the other died at a very early age. Another died at the tragic age of 18 years, while serving at a London Club. Seven of us served in the First World War. Fred the youngest the present professional at Burnham, missed it because of age. He was caught up in the second war.

Farming and golf were the only industries in our tiny village, if golf can be called an industry. It still plays a large part in the economy of the place; the links attract golfers from all over the country. Our cottage stood about 200 yards from what was then the 12th fairway, now the 15th. Between it and the links were the village green and a row of sand dunes. On the village green we kids built a little course known as 'short holes', in the sand hills another called 'long holes.'

Unlike the juniors of today, we were not encouraged to play on the links we loved. Quite the opposite, we were chased off. If in the process we were forced to leave our ball behind, that was the end of our golf until we found another, or a pal who had one to spare.

This was possibly a good thing. The more we were chased off the greater our desire to play golf on lovely greens and fairways rather than on our long and short holes where putting was a farce.

Working on the Links

Two doors from us, the Whitcombe family were born, probably the three greatest golfing brothers in history. All gained the distinction of becoming Ryder Cup players; Ernest and Charles won every national tournament of their day except The Open. Reg, the youngest, and my school pal, was the only member of the family to win this, the highest honour in golf. The long and short holes proved their worth.

In 1912 a few days before my 13th birthday I left school and began my life's work by working on the golf links. This gave me a grand opportunity for practice while walking to and from work.. Exactly three years later I left home to become an assistant to one of my elder brothers at Hendon.

Life became boring for the first year after leaving home – the war was on, little golf was being played – and the natural urge to get into uniform invited me to join the Army early. Serving with the Machine Gun Corps I was rather badly wounded just four days before the Armistice was signed. Being back in a Blighty hospital helped me to get a quick demob during the early months of 1919. It was then golf in earnest began. I remember that my first two attempts at hitting the ball while on hospital leave were most unsuccessful. No contact was made.

First Post as a Pro

In 1923 I obtained my first post as a professional at a well-known Club in South Wales, Southerndown. Having had a good grounding in teaching and clubmaking at Hendon as an assistant, I was fortunate enough to make a bit of a name for myself down there.

Tournament golf was never my strong suit – temperamentally unsuited. Whether I did well or badly, I cannot honestly say I ever enjoyed a national tournament. My first effort in 1923 should have ended in success, but from sheer fright I finished third. It was the Assistants' Championship. Sectional qualifying rounds were played over all sections of the British Isles, the qualifiers competing over 36 holes in the final. At the end of the first round I led the field and, but for missing three of the shortest possible putts in the afternoon, I would have won.

In 1928 four of us brothers were competing in the Open at Royal St George's, in Sandwich. All of us qualified for the Championship proper, a record I believe. I have forgotten which of the four finished nearer the top, it definitely was not me or I would have remembered.

While in South Wales I played a certain amount of exhibition golf, not as nerve-racking as tournament golf. One round I remember was at the Barry Golf Club. Round in 68 I broke the record for the course and have since heard the card discoloured with age, remained on the notice board with my picture until the Club was disbanded a few years ago.

I think it was in 1927 when Bert Hodson and I played two of our most famous professional golfers of those days, Abe Mitchell and George Duncan, at Southerndown. Bert was the Welsh Champion and later became a Ryder Cup player. We were beaten by two and one in a grand fourball match. Thanks to the cheers from my supporters, and there must have been a thousand of them, I got over my nerves after a few holes and played the game of my life.

Marriage and with a couple of youngsters to support my moment of decision came in 1930 when I was invited to join Calcot Park. It was a decision we have never regretted, nearly 36 years of friendship and happiness.

Golf was not so popular in those days and for a number of years life was a bit of a struggle. To add to our difficulties the second war came. With the invaluable help of my wife and our eldest daughter we took complete charge of the Club with Lady Greenly as our Honorary Secretary. We worked hard but enjoyed the experience.

I have few regrets but there is one; if I could have life over again, I would keep a record of all the Clubs I have visited, my few minor successes in tournament golf both before the war and during my golfing career since, together with the dates and courses on which I have done a Hole in One.

Treasured Prize

Fourteen times I have been lucky. My first hole in one was at Burnham in my very early days, the 14th at Camberley in 1959 when playing with my Captain, Mr N E Padwick, in the annual Captains and professional competition – curiously enough at their 14th hole. Incidentally we won this event in 1956 when I had Mr Stewart Hill to assist me. Mr Padwick also came close to giving me my second win.

The particular competitions I always enjoyed were the Alliance meetings. Playing with one of my members in competitive golf has given me a great deal of pleasure; particularly on the numerous occasions over the years we have been the winners.

One prize I treasure more than any other is the replica of the old *Reading Standard* Trophies, now taken over by the *Evening Post*, competed for at the July meeting of the Alliance, they are presented to the best amateur and professional partnership on that day. With Mr Leonard Spratt as my partner we won them in 1953, the first year they were competed for. I wish I could remember our scores, they were pretty good over the 36 holes.

Early in the tournament season of 1957 I was having dinner with Bobby Locke, who promised to play in our annual professional and lady foursomes if I could arrange that we played together. Fourteen days before, I was taken into hospital for an immediate operation. Four days before the competition was due to be played I was listening to the radio from a hospital bed about his success in the Open at St Andrews. Naturally I was denied the privilege of playing with the Open Champion. My nephew Arthur took my place and won the event with Mrs Hallaran.

Appearing on television two hours later, Bobby had to rush back to London, but made time to tell me how impressed he was with the magnificent golf Arthur had played.

At the request of Mrs Stella Cave, the Captain of the Berkshire County Ladies Association, who, as ladies do, worked so hard for their association, I raised a team of local professionals to play the county ladies to give them strong opposition before their county season began.

One of the games was impossible because of snow, but it is a match I very much hope will continue for many years. I cannot remember the handicapping on the first occasion but I do remember my team were up in arms at the end of the morning foursomes when they were down by 4½ to 1½. The eventual result was thrilling after a pep talk at lunchtime. It all depended on the last game, won by the professionals on the last green, giving my team a win eight games to seven.

In these days of big prize money, tournament professionals can win a lot of money quickly, but the lives of club professionals have greater rewards. Winning the hearts of their members is more important than money. This was brought home to me in 1955. After 25 years service my wife and I were presented with a cheque for £450 at the Great Western Hotel in Reading, subscribed to by the officials and members of my Club and presented by the late Mr John Pole, who, I am grateful to say, numbered me among his friends.

More members expressed a wish to attend this function than could be seated, so the lady members organised an 'overflow' a week or two later in the old Clubhouse. My wife was presented with a clock and I received an illuminated address, which has been hanging in my showroom for the past 13 years. It is worth more than money to ourselves and our children. My wife and I have been fortunate in attending many golfing functions together. These were two of the happiest evenings of our lives.

Of course I loved playing golf in my younger days and have been thrilled with my few moderate successes, but over the years I have gained more enjoyment and probably more success in teaching the game.

Rewards

Hard work is the lot of a club professional, but looking back on life there is no sensation quite so thrilling as the feeling of elation when you know you have given others pleasure. Teaching is a mixture of elation and frustration. Every golfer has experienced these feelings; his coach thrives or suffers in the same way. Many times I have gone home at the end of a long day feeling as though I was walking on air. Only too often, when nothing has gone right, like bursting into tears.

Starting a junior from the beginning, watching his play and swing improve and see him in the Oxford and Cambridge match a few years later makes one proud of the effort that has been successful. Three times this has happened to me. In my old age I shall be watching the career of young John Cook my latest protégé.

Enjoyment

Every day teaching of the average club golfer can be even more rewarding, noting the expressions of delight on their faces when they know their golf is improving, listening to their thrilling tales after a good round in competition. I have never found these tales boring. The fact of their reminiscing proves their enjoyment. I am just as happy to listen.

One date I shall always remember is July 7 1938, the day I visited Alexandra Palace for the first time to rehearse a show to be put on television that evening – *A Lesson on Golf.* To be the first professional to televise golf instruction made me proud, but more than a little scared. In those early days it was pretty hot in July with all those big and powerful lights around you in the one huge studio.

However, it must have been a satisfactory lesson, I was booked for a series of eight which, as far as I can remember ended in 1939 when signs of war were getting obvious. Conditions in the studio were very different in 1957, the next time I televised on a different aspect of golf. A comfortable chair and no excessive heat.

My first experience in the administrative side of golf came in 1935 when I was elected a member of the Executive Committee of the Professional Golfers Association. The dual job of Club Secretary and Club Professional immediately after the war forced me to resign from the Executive in 1946 through pressure of work at home.

Chairman

Chairman of the PGA in 1950 and professional at the Berkshire Club, Arthur Lacey, approached me with a request to help form a committee of the Southern Section and to serve on that committee. To my great surprise I was elected Chairman at their first meeting, my proudest moment to date, and re-elected back on the executive to represent the Southern Section.

Each of the next three years I was re-elected their Chairman. Even to touch on all that happened during those four years would take too much space, but I can say, with tremendous help from my colleagues, we set the Section off on a firm foundation.

It will interest all golfers to know that at the last annual meeting of the Southern Section, Bill Young of Sonning was elected chairman of committee, a position he will fill with pride and effort.

When I first served on the executive in 1935 it never crossed my mind I would one day be occupying the chair that looked to me like a throne. It happened in 1956 when I was elected chairman of the PGA. I was so scared I could scarcely sign the minutes.

Re-elected

Re-election in 1957 – unusual in those days – I felt very honoured and not nearly so scared. They were exciting days with a certain amount of turmoil, as there is bound to be in a healthy association of 1,800 members.

My proudest moment came in 1960. This year I was elected captain, the highest honour that can be conferred on any professional, the boss of the association. I have had a lot of luck in life and I am grateful.

One such stroke of luck was being chairman in 1957, the year our team won the Ryder Cup matches at Lindrick. On arrival, both teams and officials assembled and stayed at Grosvenor House for one night. That afternoon we paid a visit to the grave of Harry Vardon at Totteridge; in the evening we dined at the Guildhall, leaving for Sheffield the next morning. Spending more than a week with both teams and having a police escort to the Club each day, was quite something.

For me to attempt to describe adequately the closing stages is impossible. It was the first and only time I saw my great friend, the late Alf Padgham in tears. Soon after the matches were over I was privileged to have the Ryder Cup in my possession for about a couple of months and exhibit it at local courses and functions. Made of gold it is a valuable trophy and, sentimentally, quite irreplaceable. It lived under my bed at night and I was relieved when the time came for it to be returned to the PGA offices.

My year of Captaincy happened to coincide with the Centenary Open Championship, played at St, Andrews. As Captain of the PGA, I had the supreme honour of being invited to the Centenary Dinner held in the Clubhouse immediately before the Championship. Only thirty-two others were invited, I felt very important. With the exception of Arnold Palmer (and myself) every professional present had won The Open at least once. W Aucterlonie (1893), George Duncan (1920); Jock Hutchinson (1921); Arthur Havers (1923); Gene Sarazen (1932); Henry Cotton (1934); Alf Padgham (1936); Dick Burton (1939); Fred Daly (1947); Max Faulkner (1951); Peter Thomson (1954); Gary Player (1959).

Although completely out of my depth as a golfer, I spent a most enjoyable evening with a crowd of friendly chaps. Sitting on one side of me at dinner was Provost R Leonard and Arnold Palmer on the other. Arnie is one of the most delightful professional golfers it has been my pleasure to meet. After this dinner I saw a lot of him on the course during the championship and was disappointed when he lost by one stroke to Kel Nagle, despite a last round of 68. Arnie won in 1963.

As a very ordinary club professional I can boast of having dined at the Guildhall with the Ryder Cup teams and in the Clubhouse at St Andrews on the occasion of the Centenary Open Championship Dinner. Not that I wish to boast, no one realises more than I do that it was sheer luck on both occasions.

Their Loyalty

One more honour that came my way in 1960 was to captain a team of leading professionals against a team of leading amateurs captained by that charming gentleman, Charles Lawrie. The amateurs had scored well in the Open a month or so previous to these matches and fully expected to win. The matches were played at Prestwick.

What struck me was the loyalty of the professionals who were getting nothing for their efforts. They were out on the course early in the morning working hard during the two practise days, not taking the games lightly and giving the impression it was an honour to be playing. We held a meeting to arrange the partnerships for the foursomes on the first day and the order of play in the singles on the second day.

At the end of nine holes in the first round of the foursomes we were down in every match. Peter Mills said, "Come on, our Captain is worried, let us get stuck into them." The final result was we won the foursomes 4 - 1 and the singles 7 - 3. I still have some letters from my team.

Through all these years the officials and members of my Club never once voiced a word of complaint at my continued absence when I should have been at home taking care of their requirements.

Soon after we came to Reading I was asked to serve on the Committee of the Berks & Bucks Alliance and have remained a member of that committee throughout the years.

The Alliance died a natural death during the war years. After the war Stanley Haynes, then professional at Maidenhead, wrote to me and a few of the older members with a view of getting it going again. It is largely through his efforts local golfers still enjoy their monthly meetings.

Standing left to right: Tom Haliburton, Dai Rees, George Low, David Snell and Sid Scott.
Seated: Fred Boobyer, Peter Mills, Ernest Bradbeer, Ken Bousfield, Bernard Hunt and Peter Butler.

The Golf Foundation in its early years asked the PGA for professional representation on their committee. Another pleasant task that came my way was the additional honour of serving on their council a few years later.

Professionals' Week was my baby. I started it in the hope of raising £1,000 annually for the funds of this voluntary organisation that works so hard in the interests of junior golf. During each of the last four years more than £3,000 has been collected.

Happiest Years

Being forced to give up these various activities makes me sad but they leave me with memories of things I have enjoyed. From 1930 to 1968 have been the happiest years of our lives and I want to extend our grateful thanks to all my members, past and present, together with perhaps thousands of golfers from other Clubs who have helped in making them that way.

Born in humble circumstances, fortune has been kind to me. I can number among my friends members of the community from the highest to the most humble. The game of golf has done this for me.

The late Lord Brabazon, president of the Professional Golfers Association for many years up to the time of his death some three years ago, always welcomed me as one of his greatest friends. With a brain far bigger than mine, he was always willing to discuss matters and take advice regarding professional golf, a subject that keenly interested him. He will be remembered by many golfers for his speeches at the PGA dinners.

Worthwhile Efforts

At the other end of the scale I enjoy the visits of a man I knew as a caddie at Southerndown, now living in London. He obviously likes seeing me or he would not go to the trouble and expense of coming down. I appreciate his visits and hope they will continue

Being a club professional may be hard work, but his efforts are worthwhile from every angle. Nothing can take the place of real friends. I believe I have many among my members.

Now the time is approaching for me to retire from a Club that means so much to me; a Club that made me an honorary member more than 30 years ago. When that time comes, it will not be from choice or pressure, solely from ill health. My board of directors and members are extremely kind, I only wish it was the beginning of a long term of service, not the end.

It had always been my hope that my nephew Arthur Bradbeer would take over from me. Death has intervened. He had been a wonderful servant to me and the Club for 32 years – loyal, popular, modest and efficient, I am sure he would have more than filled my shoes. He was more than a nephew to us; his untimely end has brought with it considerable grief.

Before ending, I must pay tribute to my wife. Since we were married in 1924 she has always been affectionately referred to by me as the 'Old Girl', much to the disgust of a number of my newer lady members, not used to the term. She can certainly be numbered among the best. Without her help during the war years and since, we could not have served the Club as efficiently as I hope we have. Talking over my retirement, with members, many of them have said: "I hope the Old Girl will still be with us?" Words I have been delighted to hear. We are blessed with three children who delight in doing anything for us (she is worthy of that attention) and four loving grandchildren.

My hopes for the future are to be able to spend a considerable amount of time in the company of my members and occasionally to help my old friends with their golf. Completely severing my connections with Calcot Park and all local golf would make me most unhappy.

My Last Wish

I was reminded a few days ago of something that happened when I did my last hole-in-one. Standing on the 14th tee at Camberley I had an argument with my caddie as to which club I should take. Accepting his advice, I hit the ball. Obviously it went into the hole by the standing ovation from the spectators who were sitting behind the green. My remark to the caddie was, "Now look what you have @$#*&* well done for me!"

Another spontaneous remark: While teaching at the green end of our sixth fairway one of our best players playing the hole hit a pretty bad second shot after a tremendous drive. Passing me on his way down to the green he said, "Brad you get some awful lies at the other end of this fairway." My reply was: "Yes, and you hear some at this end."

146

Golf has been a wonderful game to me. My last request is that I shall never become disassociated with the game, or the Club I have grown to love, Calcot Park.

Ernest Bradbeer
Calcot Park Head Professional 1930 – 1968
Chairman of the PGA 1956/57
Captain of the PGA 1960

The Golfer's "If"

(With acknowledgements to Rudyard Kipling)

If you can play one day with skill and science
And find the next your game has gone to pot
And yet plod on with sturdy self-reliance
And play to win with every single shot.

If you can take the turf and open air way
To clear the cobwebs from a worried brain;
If, you can lie in rough or on the fairway,
You simply do your best and don't complain.

If you can see your faults and toil to mend them
Knowing the only mender must be you,
If you can try the wrong ways and transcend them
And when you've found the right one – follow through.

In short, if head and hands and eye do all the ruling
With temper left discarded on the shelf.
You've got the basis of a golfer's schooling
And not so bad a stance for Life itself.

"Peter Niblick" (C B K)

"The Modern Golf Professional"

(with apologies to the late W S Gilbert)

I am the very model of a modern Golf Professional
I'll sell you balls with 'lattice' marks or 'mesh' or else 'recess'-ional
I'll make you any club you like from drivers down to runners up
And show you how to use them and pitch some perfect stunners up
     I'm always giving lessons, I'm a sort of moral vitamin.
I'll teach you when you're putting, not to trickle but to hit 'em in
     My pupils never slice or pull in fact I'm always wàrning 'em
     To obviate the habit of a Craddock or a Barmingham;
     And when you're getting weary, just to vary the monotony
I'm quite prepared to hear your other troubles, if you've got any.
     In fact, as recipient of everyone's confessional.
I am the very model of a modern Golf Professional.

     I'll show you how it's easy to go out in thirty-two
     No matter if the lies are bad or if the weathers dirty too
For when you've had a guinea's worth you'll challenge a comparison
With masters of the game like Bobby Jones or Gene Sarazen
     And after all the main thing is (perhaps it is a platitude)
     To try to look the Golfer and strike the Golfer's attitude.
So when perhaps you miss the ball they'll say, if there's a crowd about,
"He's got the Bradbeer hallmark, and that's something to be proud about".
So when you're feeling down and out and rather near to suicide
     And life and golf present you not a rosy but a blue-y-side.
     Remember that not only am I a Golf Professional
     But also the recipient of everyone's confessional.

Major C B Krabbé